Joined by Grace

D0109517

"This book is a greatly needed resource for young couples. It contains basic Catholic prayers with explanations that are presented in a warm and personal style. It is more than a prayer book. It is an invitation to prayer. I am confident that this book will be a source of blessings and inspiration for all who read it."

Most Rev. David R. Choby
Bishop of Nashville

"Praying together as a family is the most important thing you will ever do. Read this book and you'll know why."

Jon Leonetti
Catholic radio host and author of *Your God Is Too Boring*

"Authentic intimacy comes from the joining of spouses' souls as well as their hearts. Prayer is how you put them together. Teri and John Bosio's book is the perfect resource for couples who want to become spiritually one."

Alice Heinzen
Director of Family Life
Diocese of La Crosse

"This book gathers prayers and practices that have sustained Catholic families for generations. It contains everything a couple needs to build their life together around a faithful connection to God. Here is a great little prayer book for couples just starting out."

Josh and Stacey Noem
Catholic bloggers at *ForYourMarriage.org*

"The apostles asked Jesus, 'Lord teach us how to pray.' John and Teri Bosio have compiled a wonderful Catholic prayer book for engaged and newlywed couples to guide them through their journey of faith and teach them to pray. It is a book every engaged couple should have!"

Deacon Tom Samoray
Family Life Director
Diocese of Nashville

"This book does a beautiful job explaining what Catholics believe about prayer and why we believe it. This is a very helpful guide for both Catholic couples and couples of mixed religious backgrounds. *Joined by Grace* will be a gift my wife and I give all couples we help prepare for marriage."

Deacon Paul Taylor
St. Frances Cabrini Catholic Church
Lebanon, Tennesee

Joined by Grace

John and Teri Bosio

A CATHOLIC PRAYER BOOK FOR ENGAGED AND NEWLY MARRIED COUPLES

AVE MARIA PRESS AVE Notre Dame, Indiana

© 2017 by John and Teri Bosio

Founded in 1865, Ave Maria Press is a ministry of the United States Province of Holy Cross.

www.avemariapress.com

Paperback: ISBN-13 978-1-59471-727-7

E-book: ISBN-13 978-1-59471-728-4

Cover and text design by K. H. Bonelli and Katherine J. Ross.

Printed and bound in the United States of America.

Library of Congress Cataloging-in-Publication Data is available.

A few minutes can be found each day
to come together before the living God,
to tell him our worries,
to ask for the needs of our family,
to pray for someone experiencing difficulty,
to ask for help in showing love,
to give thanks for life and for its blessing,
and to ask Our Lady
to protect us beneath her maternal mantle.
With a few simple words,
this moment of prayer can do immense
good for families.

—Pope Francis
The Joy of Love (*Amoris Laetitia*), 318

Contents

Part 3: Devotions

Acknowledgments

Additional Prayer Resources

A Note from the Authors

This simple prayer book was prepared to help you and your spouse discover the benefits of prayer for your marriage, whether you pray alone or together. Prayer has been part of our relationship since we were engaged, and it continues to sustain our marriage today, more than forty years later. We think of prayer as the key that opens the door of our hearts to welcome God so that we can visit and speak with him as we would with a friend. Because of this encounter with God, through prayer we find hope and courage during difficult times. We find guidance when we do not know what to do. And we find the words to express our gratitude to God for his many blessings. Prayer makes us ready to receive God's graces that help our marriages grow.

When you married in the Church, you did so in the presence of God: Father, Son, and Holy Spirit, who joined the two of you as husband and wife. The Father embraced you with his love; Christ joined your marriage to his redemptive work and is for you the model of loving; and the Holy Spirit became your guide and is the source of your spiritual strength.

As Pope Francis reminds us, God is always present in our relationships, whether we are aware of him or not. Even when you are struggling and God is not on your mind, know that he is there, standing by you, eager to show you the way, and ready to help you pick yourself up when you fall.

In this book we share with you prayers that have been helpful to us and prayers that have been part of our Catholic tradition for generations. We hope they will assist you in developing a relationship with God and that they will lead you to mature in love for your spouse. May you find in marriage the comfort and the joy that both your hearts desire.

With prayers for your marriage,
John and Teri Bosio

Getting Started

This prayer book is like a menu in a restaurant. A menu offers many options for nourishing meals. You choose what is most appealing to you at one particular moment. It may be a simple dish or a full meal, depending on your need, your hunger, the time you have available, and how much you are willing to spend. In a restaurant, you consider how much money you are willing to spend. With prayer, you must consider what it will cost you to grow closer to God and to your spouse. You should also consider what it might cost not to grow closer to God through prayer.

This book can help you on your spiritual journey. It offers you information about how Catholics pray, and it provides many of the Church's most common traditional prayers. It offers suggestions on how to pray and establish regular habits of prayer.

St. Augustine once wrote, "My heart is restless until it rests in you." We all feel a hunger for God. We hunger to know that there is someone greater than us, who is wiser, who cares for us, and who wants to help us. We often ignore this hunger because of the rush of daily life and the noise that fills our days. Yet the hunger for God is there, and we need to tend to it. Prayer helps us satisfy that hunger. Prayer helps us get to know God and learn how to accept the abundant, unending love we find in him.

To introduce prayer into your life as a couple, it is important to develop daily or weekly habits that allow you to pause whatever you are doing, quiet the noise, and remember God. From the very start of our relationship, Teri and I made it a habit to go to Mass together each Sunday and to pray each day before meals. In addition, we each have developed individual habits for spending time with God.

Regardless of how you and your spouse choose to pray, prayer will help you grow spiritually. Such spiritual growth will be reflected in the quality of your relationship, because in prayer we experience God's love, and from him we learn to love one another.

First Steps

Our Catholic tradition tells us that the family is the fundamental cell of society and of the Church. Each family, each home, is the Church in miniature; it is the place where the Gospel is taught and practiced. God resides there, and prayers are offered to him. The family is the domestic church. Before you dig into developing a richer prayer life, here are a few ideas about how to make your home more conducive to prayer so that your domestic church might flourish.

Make Your House a Sacred Space

In developing a Christian lifestyle that is enriched by prayer, the place to start is in the way you decorate your house—the home of your domestic church. Decorating your home with religious art, such as with crucifixes or images of Mary or the saints, or placing a Bible in a corner with a candle will constantly remind you that God lives there with you. These reminders are invitations to speak to God about your daily needs and to thank him for your blessings.

When John and I moved to Nashville, the kitchen of our new home had a multipurpose island. I decorated it with a plant, a candle, and a small icon of Mary that John had purchased for me in Russia while on a business trip. I made it a habit to light the candle when anyone asked me to pray for them and for our own special intentions.

I lit the candle when John traveled and when Laura, our youngest daughter, went out in the evenings. If she came home late, we would leave a note: "Laura, blow out the candle. It is lit for you."

At the time Laura was in high school, and many of her friends were not Catholic. One day she asked, "Do you know how weird this looks?" I was a little surprised that she might be embarrassed by our custom and explained that these religious symbols represent who we are.

Years later during one of Laura's visits home from college, John and I were out one evening. When we returned home, we found the candle lit with a note that said, "Mom and Dad, please blow out the candle. It is lit for you." To this day both our daughters call or text to ask us to light the candle and to pray for their intentions.

Surround Yourself with Positive Things

The environment in which we live includes the music we listen to in our homes or in the car; the books, articles and blogs we read; the TV shows and movies we watch; the sites we visit on the Internet; what we post on social media; the electronic games we play; and more. Create an environment around you that is positive and a constant reminder to you and to the people who come in contact with you that you have a relationship with God—you are a child of God.

Stop right now, at least mentally, to take inventory of what you have in your home that reminds you of God and what might exist in your environment that is not as positive as you would like. What can you change to shift toward God?

Find the Right Time

You may find yourselves wondering when you can find time to pray. We have friends who are early risers, and they pray first thing in the morning. We know others with long commutes to work who use that time for prayer. Some pray the Rosary (see pages 85–95), while others pray the Liturgy of the Hours (see pages 8–9) using prayer apps. Some read scripture or spiritual reflections during breaks at work or stop by a church to pray. Young parents pray when they can, some use soothing inspirational music to create an environment for quiet prayer. Still others end their day with a prayer, individually or as a couple. Each person has a preference. Discover yours.

Make Prayer a Habit

To create prayer habits and to reinforce them, you can remind yourself of God's presence in your life by placing a magnet on your refrigerator, a sticky note at your desk or in your car, a holy card in a book that you are reading, or a candle in your kitchen. Use reminders that work for you. These are invitations to prayer. Prayer is not a chore; it is a conversation with a friend.

Whether alone or together with your spouse, you can speak to God in prayer as you would to a friend, using your own words, or you can recite a favorite traditional prayer. Looking through this book, you will find prayer suggestions for various times and many needs.

Pray with Your Spouse and for Your Spouse

There are different ways of praying together. Some are easier than others, such as going to Mass together, praying before meals, and praying the Rosary or novenas together. These prayers are easier because they do not expose our intimate conversations with God. On the other hand, praying aloud in front of your spouse using your own words to express your feelings as you speak to God may be more difficult for some. We believe that praying together is one of the most intimate experiences a couple can share. It is a joint experience that builds your communion.

In our relationship, John and I started with the easier ways to pray as a couple. We started by praying the Our Father together. In the same way, you should start with a form of prayer that is comfortable to you, but pray. Pray together for your common intentions, and pray individually for each other, especially during those days when your relationship is under stress.

Join the Church in Worshiping

One of the most important habits in the prayer life of a couple is going to Mass each Sunday. If your spouse is not Catholic, invite him or her to accompany you to Mass as a religious activity that you do together for the benefit of your marriage and one day for your children, should you be so blessed.

Regular Mass attendance will strengthen not only your relationship with God but also your relationship with your spouse. Participation in the Eucharist transforms us as individuals and as couples. Pope Francis explained this in an address at St. Peter's on June 22, 2014, "Each time we take part in the Mass . . . the presence of Jesus and the Holy Spirit acts in us, shapes our heart, and gives us the interior attitudes that shape our behaviors according to the Gospel."

Keep This Book Close By

We mentioned earlier that this prayer book is like a menu that you find in a restaurant. It is one that you can use to satisfy your spiritual hunger, choosing from its pages those prayers, practices, or devotions that you find most satisfying along your spiritual journey toward God and into closer relationship with your spouse.

In part 1 we review how Catholics pray and the different types of prayer that are part of our Catholic tradition. We placed this at the beginning so that, in learning about the various forms of Catholic prayer, you might identify the ones with which you are most comfortable and learn to use them. It's often good to start with the simple things.

In part 2 we collect some of the Church's most common traditional prayers. These are divided into smaller groupings to help you navigate the rich collection of Catholic prayers. With each prayer, we have included a brief history and a short explanation about how and when it is commonly prayed.

Part 3 contains a selection of the spiritual practices, rituals, and prayers that have been used by Catholics across the centuries and are known as "devotions." We explain the origins of each as best as we can know them and guide you on how to pray with these treasures of our Church.

Part 1

The Ways Catholics Pray

Every family has traditions for celebrating special events such as birthdays, holidays, new beginnings, and significant accomplishments. These traditions are passed from one generation to the next, usually with adaptations along the way. For people of faith, family traditions include ways of praying. These too are handed down from grandparents and parents to younger generations.

When Teri and I married, we brought to our relationship prayer traditions from both our families. One such tradition, which we incorporated into our marriage, came from Teri's maternal grandparents. They chose St. Catherine of Siena to be the patron saint for their family. A patron saint is a role model and someone to whom we pray, asking for his or her intercession on our behalf. When Teri's parents married, they kept the tradition and chose St. Martin de Porres as the patron saint for their family. They prayed to St. Martin at the end of the blessing before meals, using the simple invocation "St. Martin, pray for us." When Teri and I married, we chose St. John the Baptist as the patron saint for our family, and so we end our blessing before meals with the invocation "St. John, pray for us."

Such are family traditions. In our case, when our families gather for a meal the recitation of the blessing becomes a unique experience. We all recite the same prayer in unison, but we end the prayer with each family invoking their patron saint, all at the same time. This sounds chaotic and can be confusing for the casual guest, but it is one that is certain to make God and the saints in heaven smile.

When Catholics pray, we need to remember that our prayers are always addressed to the Trinity, even when we pray to Mary or to the saints. We always pray to the Father in the name of Jesus, with the help of the Holy Spirit. When we direct our prayers to Mary and to the saints, we ask them to intercede on our behalf just as we might ask a friend to pray for us.

During the past two millennia, the Catholic Church has developed many ways of praying. We pray with words, with rituals, with gestures, and with sacred objects. We pray alone, we pray with others, and we pray with the whole Church when we participate in the Mass or other liturgical rites. We pray to praise God, to ask favors for ourselves or for the needs of others, and to thank God for his many gifts. Let's look at various types of prayer that Catholics commonly use.

Spontaneous Prayer

Spontaneous prayer is the simplest way to approach God in private or personal prayer. The desire to reach out and communicate with the Transcendent, to talk and to listen to God, is natural for all human beings. We find this desire expressed in many of the Psalms, such as this verse from Psalm 63: "O God, you are my God—it is you I seek! For you my body yearns; for you my soul thirsts" (Psalm 63:2).

Spontaneous prayer is often an informal conversation with God that flows from the heart, often moved by joy or sadness, anxiety or fear, anger or helplessness, gratitude or a deep sense of well-being, and other intense emotions. This conversation is carried on either quietly in our hearts and minds or aloud, whether we are in the presence of others or alone.

St. Thérèse of Lisieux described prayer with these words: "For me, prayer is a surge of the heart; it is a simple look turned toward heaven, it is a cry of recognition and of love, embracing both trial and joy" (*Manuscrits autobiographiques*, C 25r).

At times, spontaneous prayer is expressed in simple words, phrases, or invocations, such as, "Praise the Lord!" "Thank you Lord!" "Your will be done!" Or it may be expressed in the recitation of short prayers, such as, "Jesus, Mary, and Joseph, pray for us."

Spontaneous prayer is not a one-way conversation. We must also pause to listen for God's response: his quiet and gentle whisper or sometimes his loud and urgent call. It is through this heartfelt dialogue that we develop a personal relationship with God and grow in the virtues of faith, hope, and love.

Scripted Prayers

The Church also encourages us to fix regular patterns of prayer that become for us important spiritual habits. To grow closer to God, we need to make time for prayer at regular moments of our days and weeks. Likewise, we need to pray together with the people closest to us and with the wider community of the Church.

There are times when we want help expressing our thoughts and feelings and when we want to pray in unison with others. These are often times for scripted prayers. Among these prayers are the traditional formulas used for centuries by the Christian community, prayers such as the Our Father, the Hail Mary, the Glory Be, and others written for particular occasions. You will find many of these in part 2 of this book.

When praying these prayers alone, especially if a prayer is new to us, we find benefit in slowly saying the words aloud. Hearing the words enriches our prayer.

Community Prayer

Catholics believe in the Communion of Saints, a community that spans all generations of believers, living and deceased, that are part of the Body of Christ, the Church. So we never pray alone, but we join our prayer with the holy ones who have gone before us in faith as well as with all Christians living today, who by virtue of being baptized and without serious sin are considered saints.

Some time ago I (John) found a tape recorder that my family sent me from Italy when I first came to the United States in 1965. I found a reel-to-reel tape and played it, hoping it would contain good memories. To my surprise I heard the clear voices of my grandmother, my uncle, my sister, my pastor, and some neighbors who had gathered to record their news for me. It was a pleasure with a touch of sadness to listen to their voices, knowing that all those on the tape, except for my sister, have passed away. The conversations and stories went on for more than thirty minutes, and then the pastor closed the tape with a request that I pray for them and a promise that they would pray for me. Then they invited me to pray with them as the day was coming to an end.

Listening to my deceased relatives pray with me and for me reminded me of the power of prayer and the fact that we are all part of a Communion of Saints. As members of the same spiritual family in union with Christ, we constantly pray for one another. That is a unique aspect of Catholic prayer. Today I continue to pray for my deceased relatives, confident that they are praying and interceding for me.

We will say more about the Communion of Saints throughout this prayer book because it is an integral part of understanding how Catholics pray.

Liturgical Prayer

Liturgical prayer is the official public prayer of the Church. It is always communal and always rooted in ritual words and actions. It has been described by theologians as a rehearsal for the Christian life because, through participating in the liturgy, we both express what we believe and receive graces necessary to live out our beliefs. Among the different forms of liturgical prayer are the celebration of the Eucharist (the Mass) and the other sacraments: Baptism, Confirmation, Reconciliation, Anointing of the Sick, Holy Orders, and Matrimony. Liturgical prayer also includes the Liturgy of the Hours, also known as the Divine office. This is the daily prayer of the Church, prayed at regular hours of each day by priests and deacons, men and women in religious communities, and also by many laypeople. The Office consists of five Hours: the Office of Readings, Morning Prayer, Daytime Prayer, Evening Prayer, and Night Prayer. Often parish communities pray a condensed version of the Hours, commonly Morning Prayer and Evening Prayer (or Vespers).

The Church's liturgy also includes other public worship services celebrated on various occasions, such as the dedication of a church or altar and the rites contained within the *Order of Christian Initiation of Adults* (RCIA), the *Order of Celebrating Matrimony*, and the *Order of Christian Funerals*.

When we participate in liturgical prayer, we pray as a spiritual family—the Mystical Body of Christ, the Communion of Saints, which includes those believers who are living, those who have died and are in purgatory, and those who are in heaven. During the liturgy it is Christ himself, the high priest, who offers worship to the Father. We are joined to him by the power of the Holy Spirit and are made holy by the graces we receive. When we participate in the Mass, we join not only our fellow Catholics in worshiping the Father but also Christ and all the angels and saints.

Praying with the Scriptures (Lectio Divina)

One of the ways Catholics pray is by reading and reflecting on the scriptures. The Bible is God's word to us. St. Ambrose explained that we should pray with the sacred scriptures so that there can be a dialogue between God and us. We listen to God speak to us, and we respond to him.

If you search the Internet about how to pray with scripture, you will find many articles with good suggestions. One approach you are likely to find is called *lectio divina,* which when translated from Latin, means "divine reading."

Lectio divina is a very simple method that has its origin among the Benedictine monks. If you are new to lectio divina and want to try this method, we suggest that you begin by praying using short passages from the New Testament. For example, you could choose an excerpt from one of the New Testament letters or one of the gospels, perhaps even the passage selected by the Church for the Mass of the day. Or you could choose to reflect on one of the Psalms. If you want to try lectio divina, follow these simple steps, which we learned from one of our pastors.

1. Go to a quiet place, intending to pray, and remind yourself that you are in God's presence. He will speak to you through his Word.

2. Read the chosen scripture passage slowly. If you can, read it aloud, listening to the sound of your voice.

3. Pause whenever a word or phrase catches your attention or moves you. Let it sink in, and become aware of how you feel. Ask God in prayer, *Why this word or phrase? What do you wish to say to me, Lord?*

4. Read the passage again. You may find that it has a fuller meaning the second time.

5. Talk to God about your experience as you would talk to your closest friend. Be honest about what you think or feel.

6. Be in God's presence, and when the time is up, recite the Lord's Prayer in gratitude.

The purpose of lectio divina is to help you experience God through the scriptures and grow closer to him by listening to his message.

Simple Rituals and Devotional Prayers

Rituals

Catholics are known for our rituals and devotions, which do indeed lie at the heart of Catholic practice. Rituals are an essential part of our human experience. Through rituals, we express our emotional and spiritual response to significant life experiences, assign meaning to these experiences, and learn to interact with each other through them. For example, when I (John) visit my family in Italy, I need to remember that their greeting ritual is different from ours in the United States. In Italy, when relatives meet, they kiss on both cheeks, which is a ritual that expresses human emotion. An example of assigning meaning through ritual in the secular realm is a presidential inauguration. Through a complex set of ritual actions, an elected official becomes president. The person's status within the nation changes as his or her role in history takes on new meaning.

Every culture, family, and religion creates and is shaped by particular rituals. Our Catholic tradition has unique rituals that reflect what we believe about God and how we relate to him. For example, Catholics make the Sign of the Cross and genuflect when entering a church. The celebrations of the sacraments are filled with ritual words and actions. Consider the Mass, for instance, during which we process, stand, kneel, bow, sing, listen, pray aloud and in silence, and watch and listen as the priest enacts a series of actions while praying scripted prayers. Rituals help us express physically what we feel and believe interiorly.

Devotions

Devotions are expressions of personal piety toward God, Mary, and the saints. They are considered personal or private prayers, whether prayed alone or with other members of one's community. Devotions are perhaps best understood as scripted prayer forms that usually contain several brief prayers (often repetitive) along with some simple ritual actions. For example, the Rosary is made up of repetitive groupings of Our Fathers and Hail Marys that are prayed while moving rosary beads through one's fingers.

Devotions are not liturgical, which means they are not a part of the official public worship of the Church, despite the common practice in many places of certain devotions being prayed within a church. Rather, devotions flow from and enhance the liturgical life of the Catholic Church.

Among the most popular devotions are the Rosary, eucharistic adoration, the Stations of the Cross, novenas, Benediction of the Blessed Sacrament, and the Angelus. These practices help us connect emotionally to the spiritual world to receive graces and to find inspiration for our lives.

Blessing and Adoration

We all experience moments when we are awestruck by the beauty of God's creation, the amazing kindness or generosity of other people, or the sheer goodness of life. At times such as these, Catholics see God. Our awe and joy lead us to turn to God in prayer and adoration, acknowledging that we are his creatures and blessing him for what he does for us.

Prayers of adoration and blessing can be spontaneous expressions of our heart, scripted prayers, passages from the Bible, or prayers we say as a Church community in the liturgy. One common prayer of adoration and blessing is the first two verses of Psalm 103: "Bless the Lord, my soul; all my being, bless his holy name! Bless the Lord, my soul; and do not forget all his gifts."

John and I live in a house that backs up to a farm. Some mornings, looking out of our windows at the farm and seeing cows grazing or deer and coyotes running across the field leads us to think about God and the beauty of the world he created. We turn to God and adore him for the wonder of creation. Through prayers of blessing and adoration, we affirm God's goodness and the many rich blessings that flow from him.

Petition

As in any relationship, in our interactions with God we often ask for favors. Sometimes we ask gently, and sometimes we beg and implore. When we turn to God asking for help, we recognize that we are sinners and that we need his help and forgiveness.

Catholics believe that our prayers of petition cannot stand alone as selfish requests. When we pray, we ask God for help with the expectation that God will give us what he knows we need. Our prayers of petition need to be anchored by our openness to God's will, whatever it may be.

I (John) remember clearly my prayers during a period of six months, years ago, after I was laid off due to downsizing. I was looking for a job; money and insurance coverage were running out. In my daily prayers I had to remind myself that God knew best what I needed and would provide it in his own time and that I just needed to do my part.

We pray knowing that the Father will give us what we ask, when and if it is part of his providential design. Jesus encouraged us to pray and to ask what we need of the Father in his name. "And whatever you ask in my name, I will do, so that the Father may be glorified in the Son" (John 14:13).

Intercession

We read in the letter of James: "Pray for one another, that you may be healed. The fervent prayer of a righteous person is very powerful" (James 5:16). Our prayer is intercession when instead of praying for ourselves we pray for the needs of others. We pray to Christ to intercede with the Father on behalf of the people we love, whether alive or dead.

As we write, two very dear friends are in hospice care after years of battling cancer. They are on our minds, and we are praying for them—that they feel the comfort of God's presence in this moment of their lives. These are prayers of intercession.

Intercession can best be understood in the context of the Church's belief in the Communion of Saints, which is a tenet of our faith that is professed in the Apostles' Creed. The Communion of Saints is the community of all those who are united in Christ: those who are living and those who have passed away. We are all one big spiritual family, and we pray for one another's needs to the Father through Christ with the help of the Holy Spirit. For me (Teri), it is comforting to think that my mother, who passed away in 2009, is in heaven, and when I encounter a problem I can still turn to her and ask her to pray for me.

That is why Catholics pray for and to the dead and pray to Mary and to the saints. As members of the same family of believers, we pray to Mary, our spiritual mother, to intercede for us with her Son, and similarly we pray to our favorite saints to intercede on our behalf with Jesus.

In our parishes we also pray intercessory prayers in most liturgical celebrations. During Mass, at the end of the Liturgy of the Word we offer the Universal Prayer, also known as the Prayer of the Faithful. During this prayer, the priest, the deacon, or the lector read individual intentions: we pray for the needs of the Church, the country, the community, the sick, the poor, the needs of those present, and so on. After each petition we respond, "Lord, hear our prayer."

Thanksgiving

Gratitude is an important attitude in life. Gratitude toward the people in our lives—spouses, friends, neighbors, the peoples we encounter while going about our daily activities—strengthens our relationships with them. It helps us appreciate what they have done for us. Our words of thanks tell them that we recognize their gifts and their generosity. The same is true for our relationship with God, who is the source of all the gifts we have received. Even as we are accustomed to asking God for favors, we need also to make it a habit to express our gratitude for his blessings large and small.

Whether we give God thanks through spontaneous prayer, reciting a scripted prayer, praying a Psalm, or attending Mass, a grateful heart strengthens our relationship with God. The Mass is the Church's great public prayer of thanksgiving. In fact, the word *Eucharist* is a Greek word that means "thanksgiving."

This single verse from Psalm 118 is a beautiful and simple prayer of thanksgiving that you can memorize and make a habit of praying each day: "Give thanks to the LORD, for he is good, his mercy endures forever" (Psalm 118:1).

Praise

There is a fine distinction between prayers of blessing and adoration and prayers of praise. Through prayers of blessing and adoration, we bless God for all his gifts, while through prayers of praise, we praise God simply because he is God. An example of this type of prayer is the second verse of Psalm 146: "Praise the LORD, my soul; I will praise the LORD all my life, sing praise to my God while I live."

We recite and sing prayers of praise in the celebration of the Mass. An example is when we sing or recite the Gloria, the hymn early in the Mass that begins, "Glory to God in the highest, and on earth peace to people of good will." (See pages 50–51 for the text of the Gloria.)

The Catholic Church also teaches us that living our faith by following God's will each day is an act of praise. When we recognize God's presence in our daily lives—whether we eat, work, drive, shop, cook, take care of the children, or express our love to our spouse—our words and actions give glory to God, and they are prayer. St. Paul tells us, "Pray without ceasing" (1 Thessalonians 5:17).

Psalms, Canticles, and Litanies

Psalms

The Psalms are prayers and poems collected over several centuries in the Old Testament and originally written for use in Hebrew worship. Among the Psalms are prayers of praise and thanksgiving; cries for help, called lamentations; and prayers for different occasions. All of them express trust in God.

From the beginning of the Church the Psalms have been used as the public prayer of the Church. Today we pray with the Psalms at Mass, in the Liturgy of the Hours, and in many of the liturgical rituals of the Church such as the sacraments.

The Psalms are also wonderful for private prayer because they inspire us to pray with trust in God. They also teach us how to pray. Perhaps the most familiar is Psalm 23 because of the comfort it offers in times of trouble.

Psalm 23

The Lord is my shepherd;
    there is nothing I lack.
In green pastures he makes me lie down;
    to still waters he leads me;
    he restores my soul.
He guides me along right paths
    for the sake of his name.

Even though I walk through the valley of the
    shadow of death,
    I will fear no evil, for you are with me;
    your rod and your staff comfort me.

You set a table before me
    in front of my enemies;
You anoint my head with oil;
    my cup overflows.
Indeed, goodness and mercy will pursue me
    all the days of my life;
I will dwell in the house of the LORD
    for endless days.

We urge you to pick up a Bible and read the Psalms, find
a few favorite passages, and bookmark them. Pray these
often, keeping in mind that you join your prayer to our
ancestors in the faith, even reaching back to the faith of
the Hebrew people into which Jesus was born.

Canticles

Canticles are songs of praise found in the Bible, both in
the Old Testament and the New Testament. They exude
joy. Among the Old Testament canticles is the Canticle
of the Three Young Men in the book of Daniel (3:57–87,
89–90). The story surrounding this canticle is that of three
young men who refused to worship an idol and instead
chose death in a fiery furnace. However, the fire of the
furnace did not harm them, and from the middle of the
flames they sang their praises to God.

Canticle of the Three Young Men

Teri and I like this canticle so much that when we were building our new home, with the permission of the builder, we wrote on the bare studs of various rooms our favorite scripture passages. Among these was verse 71 from this canticle: "Nights and days, bless the Lord; praise and exalt him above all forever."

> Bless the Lord, all you works of the Lord, praise and exalt him above all forever.
>
> Angels of the Lord, bless the Lord, praise and exalt him above all forever.
>
> You heavens, bless the Lord, praise and exalt him above all forever.
>
> All you waters above the heavens, bless the Lord, praise and exalt him above all forever.
>
> All you powers, bless the Lord; praise and exalt him above all forever.
>
> Sun and moon, bless the Lord; praise and exalt him above all forever.
>
> Stars of heaven, bless the Lord; praise and exalt him above all forever.
>
> Every shower and dew, bless the Lord; praise and exalt him above all forever.
>
> All you winds, bless the Lord; praise and exalt him above all forever.
>
> Fire and heat, bless the Lord; praise and exalt him above all forever.
>
> Cold and chill, bless the Lord; praise and exalt him above all forever.

Dew and rain, bless the Lord; praise and exalt him above all forever.

Frost and chill, bless the Lord; praise and exalt him above all forever.

Hoarfrost and snow, bless the Lord; praise and exalt him above all forever.

Nights and days, bless the Lord; praise and exalt him above all forever.

Light and darkness, bless the Lord; praise and exalt him above all forever.

Lightnings and clouds, bless the Lord; praise and exalt him above all forever.

Let the earth bless the Lord, praise and exalt him above all forever.

Mountains and hills, bless the Lord; praise and exalt him above all forever.

Everything growing on earth, bless the Lord; praise and exalt him above all forever.

You springs, bless the Lord; praise and exalt him above all forever.

Seas and rivers, bless the Lord; praise and exalt him above all forever.

You sea monsters and all water creatures, bless the Lord; praise and exalt him above all forever.

All you birds of the air, bless the Lord; praise and exalt him above all forever.

All you beasts, wild and tame, bless the Lord; praise and exalt him above all forever.

All you mortals, bless the Lord; praise and exalt
  him above all forever.
O Israel, bless the Lord; praise and exalt him
  above all forever.
Priests of the Lord, bless the Lord; praise and exalt
  him above all forever.
Servants of the Lord, bless the Lord; praise and
  exalt him above all forever.
Spirits and souls of the just, bless the Lord; praise
  and exalt him above all forever.
Holy and humble of heart, bless the Lord; praise
  and exalt him above all forever.
Give thanks to the Lord, who is good,
whose mercy endures forever.
Bless the God of gods, all you who fear the Lord;
praise and give thanks,
for his mercy endures forever.

From the gospels come the Canticle of Zechariah (see
Luke 1:68–79) and the Canticle of Mary, also known as the
Magnificat (see Luke 1:46–55; see pages 56–57 for the text
of the Magnificat). These gospel canticles are used regularly at Morning Prayer and Evening Prayer, respectively.

Litanies

Litanies are prayers that consist of the repetition of a plea
to God the Father for his mercy and assistance through
the mediation of Christ and through the intercession of
the saints. An example of a litany that you may be familiar with from going to Mass is the *Kyrie, Eleison* prayer:

"Lord, have mercy; Christ, have mercy; Lord, have mercy" (see pages 49–50). There are many litanies used in private prayer, but only a few are used in the Church's liturgy. Another litany that is probably familiar to many Catholics is the Litany of the Saints, which we pray at baptisms and during the Easter Vigil. In the case of the latter, we sing the litany just before renewing our baptismal promises. We also call upon the saints with this litany during an ordination to the priesthood or at the beginning of the conclave for the election of a pope.

Other litanies that are used in the private or public prayers of the Church are the Litany of the Blessed Virgin Mary, Litany of the Holy Name of Jesus, Litany of the Sacred Heart of Jesus, Litany of the Most Precious Blood of Jesus, and the Litany to St. Joseph.

Litany of the Saints

The Litany of the Saints is a prayer to the Holy Trinity, during which we invoke the intersession of Mary, the archangels, and all the saints to pray for us. A leader proclaims or a cantor chants the names of the saints, and the congregation responds in unison: "Pray for us."

Holy Mary, Mother of God, pray for us.
St. Michael, pray for us.
Holy angels of God, pray for us.
St. Joseph, pray for us.
St. John the Baptist, pray for us.
St. Peter and St. Paul, pray for us.
St. Andrew, pray for us.

St. John, pray for us.
St. Mary Magdalene, pray for us.
St. Stephen, pray for us.
St. Ignatius of Antioch, pray for us.
St. Lawrence, pray for us.
St. Perpetua and St. Felicity, pray for us.
St. Agnes, pray for us.
St. Gregory, pray for us.
St. Augustine, pray for us.
St. Athanasius, pray for us.
St. Basil, pray for us.
St. Martin, pray for us.
St. Benedict, pray for us.
St. Francis and St. Dominic, pray for us.
St. Francis Xavier, pray for us.
St. John Vianney, pray for us.
St. Catherine, pray for us.
St. Teresa, pray for us.
All you saints of God, pray for us.

Lord, be merciful, Lord, save us.
From all harm, Lord, save us.
From every sin, Lord, save us.
From all temptations, Lord, save us.
From everlasting death, Lord, save us.
By your coming among us, Lord, save us.
By your death and rising to new life, Lord, save us.
By your gift of the Holy Spirit, Lord, save us.

Be merciful to us sinners, Lord, hear our prayer.
Guide and protect your Holy Church,
Lord, hear our prayer.
Keep our pope and all the clergy in faithful ser-
vice to your Church.
Lord, hear our prayer.
Bring all peoples together in trust and peace.
Lord, hear our prayer.
Strengthen us in your service.
Lord, hear our prayer.
Jesus, Son of the living God.
Lord, hear our prayer.
Christ, hear us. Christ, graciously hear us.
Amen.

Litany of the Holy Name of Jesus

This litany is five centuries old. Its composition is
attributed to two Franciscan friars: St. Bernardino of Siena
and St. John of Capistrano. The prayer can be recited by
groups or by individuals with the intention of asking
Jesus for his mercy.

Lord, have mercy. Lord, have mercy.
Christ, have mercy. Christ, have mercy.
Lord, have mercy. Lord, have mercy.

God our Father in heaven, have mercy on us.
God the Son, have mercy on us.

Redeemer of the world, have mercy on us.

God the Holy Spirit, have mercy on us.

Holy Trinity, one God, have mercy on us.

Jesus, Son of the living God, have mercy on us.

Jesus, splendor of the Father, have mercy on us.

Jesus, brightness of everlasting light, have mercy
on us.

Jesus, king of glory, have mercy on us.

Jesus, dawn of justice, have mercy on us.

Jesus, Son of the Virgin Mary, have mercy on us.

Jesus, worthy of our love, have mercy on us.

Jesus, worthy of our wonder, have mercy on us.

Jesus, mighty God, have mercy on us.

Jesus, father of the world to come, have mercy
on us.

Jesus, prince of peace, have mercy on us.

Jesus, all powerful, have mercy on us.

Jesus, pattern of patience, have mercy on us.

Jesus, model of obedience, have mercy on us.

Jesus, gentle and humble of heart, have mercy
on us.

Jesus, lover of chastity, have mercy on us.

Jesus, lover of us all, have mercy on us.

Jesus, God of peace, have mercy on us.

Jesus, author of life, have mercy on us.

Jesus, model of goodness, have mercy on us.

Jesus, seeker of souls, have mercy on us.

Jesus, our God, have mercy on us.

Jesus, our refuge, have mercy on us.

Jesus, father of the poor, have mercy on us.
Jesus, treasure of the faithful, have mercy on us.
Jesus, Good Shepherd, have mercy on us.
Jesus, the true light, have mercy on us.
Jesus, eternal wisdom, have mercy on us.
Jesus, infinite goodness, have mercy on us.
Jesus, our way and our life, have mercy on us.
Jesus, joy of angels, have mercy on us.
Jesus, king of patriarchs, have mercy on us.
Jesus, teacher of apostles, have mercy on us.
Jesus, master of evangelists, have mercy on us.
Jesus, courage of martyrs, have mercy on us.
Jesus, light of confessors, have mercy on us.
Jesus, purity of virgins, have mercy on us.
Jesus, crown of all saints, have mercy on us.

Lord, be merciful. Jesus, save your people.
From all evil, Jesus, save your people.
From every sin, Jesus, save your people.
From the snares of the devil,
Jesus, save your people.
From your anger, Jesus, save your people.
From the spirit of infidelity,
Jesus, save your people.
From everlasting death, Jesus, save your people.
From neglect of your Holy Spirit,
Jesus, save your people.
By the mystery of your incarnation,
Jesus, save your people.

By your birth, Jesus, save your people.
By your childhood, Jesus, save your people.
By your hidden life, Jesus, save your people.
By your public ministry, Jesus, save your people.
By your agony and crucifixion,
Jesus, save your people.
By your abandonment, Jesus, save your people.
By your grief and sorrow, Jesus, save your people.
By your death and burial, Jesus, save your people.
By your rising to new life, Jesus, save your people.
By your return in glory to the Father,
Jesus, save your people.
By your gift of the holy Eucharist,
Jesus, save your people.
By your joy and glory, Jesus, save your people.

Christ, hear us. Christ, hear us.
Lord Jesus, hear our prayer.
Lord Jesus, hear our prayer.
Lamb of God, you take away the sins of the world.
    Have mercy on us.
Lamb of God, you take away the sins of the world.
    Have mercy on us.
Lamb of God, you take away the sins of the world.
    Have mercy on us.

Part 2

Common Prayers

This section of *Joined by Grace* contains a collection of traditional prayers that Catholics have prayed for centuries. These are prayers that parents and grandparents have taught their children and grandchildren. They are the vehicles through which Catholic faith and spirituality have been passed on from one generation to the next. Each prayer brings with it a story, and we give you brief explanations of origins when they are known.

As you create prayer habits in your married life, some of these prayers are likely to become favorites. Some probably are already. For me (John), the Prayer to the Guardian Angel is one of the first prayers I learned as a child. I remember kneeling on my parents' bed before going to sleep and praying it from a very early age. Another prayer with special meaning for our family and for many is the Our Father. When our children were young, we would often pile up on our bed before going to sleep and together pray the Our Father after we each named our prayer intentions for the day.

Some of these essential Catholic prayers were created many centuries ago from passages of the New Testament, such as the Our Father and the Hail Mary. Others were composed in the early years of the Church, such as the Apostles' Creed and the Nicene Creed, when the Christian community was trying to define what it believed. Some have been given to us by the saints, such as the Prayer to the Holy Spirit of St. Augustine, the Peace Prayer of St. Francis, and St. Patrick's Breastplate. Among the recent prayers found in this part are those written by St. Teresa of Calcutta, St. John Paul II, and Pope Francis.

All these prayers are a treasure that captures the spiritual traditions of the Catholic Church. They are tools that we can use to grow as members of God's family, which we call the Church, and to grow in our personal relationship with the Father, the Son, and the Holy Spirit—the Holy Trinity.

The Basics

Sign of the Cross
In the name of the Father,
and of the Son,
and of the Holy Spirit.
Amen.

The Sign of the Cross is a ritual blessing used by Catholics. It is often used when beginning and ending prayer and when entering or leaving a church. Its words are sometimes spoken aloud but are often said silently to oneself. At times the gesture is slow and deliberate, and at other times it's rushed with urgency. Whatever the circumstance, making the Sign of the Cross is widely recognized as a Catholic practice.

To make the Sign of the Cross, Catholics trace a cross upon themselves with the right hand. We touch our forehead while saying, "In the name of the Father," then our chest while saying, "and of the Son," the left shoulder while saying, "and of the Holy," then the right shoulder while saying, "Spirit. Amen."

Christians have used the Sign of the Cross since the earliest centuries of the Church. It reminds us that Christ saved us through his death on the Cross and that we do all things in God's name: Father, Son, and Holy Spirit.

Glory Be
Glory be to the Father, and to the Son, and to the
Holy Spirit;

as it was in the beginning, is now,
and ever shall be,
world without end.
Amen.

The Glory Be is an ancient hymn or prayer of praise giving glory to the Blessed Trinity. It is a beautiful expression of our faith in the equality of Father, Son, and Holy Spirit. Also known as the Gloria Patri, this simple prayer has been used in the Church since the early centuries and imitates St. Paul's expressions of praise found in his letter to the Romans: "For from him and through him and for him are all things. To him be glory forever. Amen" (Romans 11:36).

Today the Glory Be is commonly used after praying the Psalms in the Liturgy of the Hours, after each decade of the Rosary, in novenas, and in other Catholic devotions.

Our Father (The Lord's Prayer)

Our Father, who art in heaven,
hallowed be thy name;
thy kingdom come;
thy will be done on earth as it is in heaven.
Give us this day our daily bread;
and forgive us our trespasses
as we forgive those who trespass against us;
and lead us not into temptation,
but deliver us from evil.
Amen.

The Our Father, also known as the Lord's Prayer, is another one of our oldest prayers. We find its original words in the New Testament, in the Gospel of Matthew (Matthew 6:5–13) and in the Gospel of Luke (Luke 11:1–4). Jesus himself gave us this prayer in response to a request from one of his disciples, who asked, "Lord, teach us to pray." This prayer is common to all Christians, with some slight variations. For instance, in many places a doxology is prayed at the end of the prayer: "For thine is the kingdom, and the power, and the glory, for ever and ever. Amen." In other Christian communities, this doxology is rarely if ever added. As Catholics we add the doxology after the Our Father during Mass.

Hail Mary

Hail Mary, full of grace, the Lord is with you;
blessed are you among women,
and blessed is the fruit of your womb, Jesus.
Holy Mary, Mother of God,
pray for us sinners
now and at the hour of our death.
Amen.

The Hail Mary is a traditional Catholic prayer to Mary, the mother of Jesus, our Lord. The Hail Mary begins with two greetings to Mary. The first comes from the angel Gabriel when he announced to Mary that God had chosen her to be the mother of his Son. Gabriel said, "Hail, favored one! The Lord is with you" (Luke 1:28).

The other salutation comes from her cousin Elizabeth, the mother of John the Baptist. When Mary visited Elizabeth, she said to Mary, "Blessed are you among women, and blessed is the fruit of your womb" (Luke 1:42).

The second part of the Hail Mary—"Holy Mary, Mother of God . . ."—was a plea added later to ask for Mary's prayers on our behalf. The prayer has been widely used in the Catholic Church and is the central prayer of the Rosary and of the Angelus.

The Apostles' Creed

I believe in God,
the Father almighty,
Creator of heaven and earth,
and in Jesus Christ, his only Son, our Lord,
who was conceived by the Holy Spirit,
born of the Virgin Mary,
suffered under Pontius Pilate,
was crucified, died, and was buried;
he descended into hell;
on the third day he rose again from the dead;
he ascended into heaven,
and is seated at the right hand of God the Father
    almighty;
from there he will come to judge the living and
    the dead.
I believe in the Holy Spirit,
the holy catholic Church,
the Communion of Saints,
the forgiveness of sins,

the resurrection of the body,
and life everlasting.
Amen.

The Apostles' Creed is a statement of our faith. It captures in twelve short statements what Christians believe. A legend dating back to the fourth century reports that under the influence of the Holy Spirit each of the twelve apostles contributed a statement. In the Catholic Church, this creed is sometimes used during Mass in place of the Nicene Creed. It is also used at the beginning of the recitation of the Rosary.

In a question and answer form, this creed is used at baptisms when the minister asks those to be baptized, "Do you believe in God, the Father almighty, Creator of heaven and earth?" All answer, "I do!" The minister continues with more questions based on the words of the creed.

Daily Prayers

St. Paul wrote to the early Christians in Ephesus, "With all prayer and supplication, pray at every opportunity in the Spirit" (Ephesians 6:18). And so Catholics are encouraged to pray throughout the day. Pope Francis writes in *The Joy of Love*, "Every morning, on rising, we reaffirm before God our decision to be faithful, come what may in the course of the day. And all of us, before going to sleep, hope to wake up and continue this adventure, trusting in the Lord's help" (319).

On Waking
This is the day the LORD has made;
let us rejoice in it and be glad.

–Psalm 118:24

This prayer, a verse from Psalm 118, is a wonderful way to start the day upon waking. It offers praise to God and reminds us to be thankful for the blessings we will encounter during the day.

Morning Offering
O Jesus, through the Immaculate Heart of Mary,
I offer you my prayers, works, joys,
and sufferings of this day
for all the intentions of your Sacred Heart,
in union with the Holy Sacrifice of the Mass
throughout the world,

for the salvation of souls, the reparation of sins,
the reunion of all Christians,
and in particular for the intentions of the Holy
Father this month.
Amen.

The Morning Offering is a prayer Catholics are encouraged to say at the beginning of the day. With this prayer, we start our daily activities by dedicating our day to Jesus. We unite ourselves to Christ and offer our suffering for the good of others.

There are several versions of the Morning Offering. The one used here is inspired by Jesus' request to St. Margaret Mary that people honor his Sacred Heart. It was written in 1844 by Fr. François-Xavier Gautrelet for his Apostleship of Prayer, which he founded that year.

Prayer before Work (Come, Holy Spirit)

Come, Holy Spirit, fill the hearts of your faithful
and kindle in them the fire of your love.
Send forth your Spirit, and they shall be created.
And you shall renew the face of the earth.

O God, who by the light of the Holy Spirit
did instruct the hearts of the faithful,
grant that by the same Holy Spirit
we may be truly wise
and ever enjoy his consolations,
through Christ our Lord.
Amen.

The Church encourages us to be aware of God through-out the day and to let the Holy Spirit guide us to know what to do and to give us the courage to do what is right. A favorite prayer for many saints has been this prayer to the Holy Spirit. This may be a good prayer to say each day before you start your work, whether you are traveling; working in an office, a shop, a plant, or a farm; or caring for your children at home. This ancient prayer has its origin in the liturgy of the Church.

Grace before Meals

Bless us, O Lord, and these your gifts
which we are about to receive from your bounty,
through Christ our Lord.
Amen.

We pray before meals (sometimes referred to as "saying Grace") to follow the example of Jesus, who prayed before eating (see Matthew 14:15–21). We say this prayer to ask God's blessings on those present and on the food we are about to eat. Reciting this prayer together as a family is a wonderful tradition that strengthens the faith of all who gather to eat. It reminds us of our need for God's blessings and to trust in God for these gifts.

Prayer after Meals

We give you thanks for all your gifts, almighty God,
living and reigning now and forever.
Amen.

Many families also say a prayer after each meal. The prayer after a meal is a prayer of thanksgiving. We thank God for all the gifts he has given us, including the food we just ate, as we acknowledge that God is eternal.

Prayer to the Guardian Angel

Angel of God, my guardian dear,
to whom God's love commits me here,
ever this day be at my side,
to light and guard, to rule and guide.
Amen.

Catholics believe that from the time of creation there have been spiritual beings created by God, which in the Bible are called angels. Angels are servants and messengers of God, announcing his salvation and serving God in carrying out his plans. Belief in guardian angels is rooted in Psalm 91:11: "For he commands his angels with regard to you, to guard you wherever you go."

The origin of the Prayer to the Guardian Angel can be traced back to the monks of the Middle Ages. The popular translation used today comes from the nineteenth century. In this prayer we ask the angel assigned to us to protect, guard, and guide us.

Catholics celebrate the Feast of the Guardian Angels each year on October 2.

The Jesus Prayer

Lord Jesus Christ, Son of God,
have mercy on me, a sinner.

The Jesus Prayer can be recited anytime during one's day. It is a prayer of humility and contrition. Although this prayer has its origins in Eastern Christianity, it reminds us of the words of the tax collector in the parable of the Pharisee and the tax collector (Luke 18:9–19). The Jesus Prayer has been repeated like a mantra by many hermits and monks in their efforts to grow closer to God with the simplest of prayers. It is an easy-to-remember yet powerful prayer that helps us stay focused on Christ all day long.

Prayer to St. Michael the Archangel

St. Michael the Archangel, defend us in battle.
Be our defense against the wickedness
and snares of the Devil.
May God rebuke him, we humbly pray,
and do you, O Prince of the heavenly hosts,
by the power of God,
thrust into hell Satan, and all the evil spirits,
who prowl about the world
seeking the ruin of souls.
Amen.

This is a prayer that is said to have been written by Pope Leo XIII. In 1884 he ordered the prayer to be said at the end of each Mass, in defense of the independence of the Vatican, which had been overtaken by Italian soldiers seeking to unify the various states on the Italian peninsula into one country: Italy.

In 1930, a year after the Vatican State was restored, Pope Pius XI ordered that the intention for which this prayer is offered should be changed. The new intention was religious freedom for the people in Russia. In 1964 the practice of reciting the Prayer to St. Michael the Archangel at the end of each Mass was discontinued, but the use of this prayer in private devotions has continued.

Pope John Paul II said during his Sunday address on April 24, 1994, "Although this prayer is no longer recited at the end of Mass, I ask everyone not to forget it and to recite it to obtain help in the battle against the forces of darkness and against the spirit of this world." With this prayer, we pray to St. Michael to help us overcome our temptations and the influence of evil in the world.

A Family Blessing at Bedtime

> May almighty God bless you
> in the name of the Father,
> and of the Son,
> and of the Holy Spirit,
> with life everlasting.
> Amen.

If and when you are blessed with children, it is a wonderful practice to bless your child or your children each night at bedtime. In a homily on Dec. 27, 2015—Feast of the Holy Family—Pope Francis emphasized the importance of parents blessing their children each day: "What can be more beautiful than for a father and mother to bless their

children at the beginning and end of each day, to trace
on their forehead the sign of the cross, as they did on the
day of their baptism? Is this not the simplest prayer which
parents can offer for their children?"

Nunc Dimittis

Antiphon:
Protect us, Lord, as we stay awake;
watch over us as we sleep, that awake
we may keep watch with Christ,
and asleep, rest in his peace.

Now, Master, you let your servant go in peace.
You have fulfilled your promise.
My own eyes have seen your salvation,
which you have prepared
in the sight of all peoples.
A light to bring the Gentiles from darkness;
the glory of your people Israel.
Glory be to the Father and to the Son
and to the Holy Spirit,
as it was in the beginning,
is now, and ever shall be,
world without end.
Amen.

Antiphon:
Protect us, Lord, as we stay awake;
watch over us as we sleep, that awake
we may keep watch with Christ,

and asleep, rest in his peace.

The *Nunc Dimittis* is based on the Canticle of Simeon from the Gospel of Luke (2:29–32) and is prayed each day as part of Compline, or Night Prayer, which marks the final hour of the Liturgy of the Hours. The canticle is preceded and followed by an antiphon that invokes the protection of God during the night. The Canticle of Simeon comes from the story of Simeon, a devout Jew who had been promised by God that he would not die before seeing the Messiah. When Mary and Joseph brought Jesus to the Temple to be consecrated to the Lord and to offer a sacrifice, as was required by the Mosaic Law, they met Simeon. Upon seeing Jesus and holding him in his arms, Simeon prayed, "Now . . . let your servant go in peace." It is from this phrase that the title *Nunc Dimittis* comes. This Latin phrase means "now, you dismiss" and is commonly rendered here as "let your servant go."

Examen

The following four-step daily examen is adapted from the writings of Fr. Stephen Wolf in *Being Spouses:*

1. Become aware of God's presence.
2. Review the day with gratitude, giving thanks to the Father for all the good you experienced.
3. Review your day, facing your shortcomings— what you did that you are sorry for, and the things you should have done but did not. Ask Jesus for mercy.

4. Review your next day, and ask the Holy Spirit
    to help you do better.

Catholics are encouraged to end each day with an evening
prayer accompanied by a brief examination of conscience
and an Act of Contrition.

One of the strong proponents of a daily examination of
conscience was St. Ignatius of Loyola, the founder of the
Jesuits, who prescribed to the members of his order that
they should do an examination of conscience twice a day.
The type of examination of conscience that St. Ignatius
encouraged is often referred to as the examen.

During the examen you review your day: how you
experienced the presence of God and the mistakes you
may have made. Some would say that this examination of
conscience is a way to check in with Jesus to hear what
he is telling us about the way we lived our day and to ask
for the graces to do better tomorrow.

Act of Contrition

O my God, I am heartily sorry
for having offended you,
and I detest all my sins
because of your just punishment,
but most of all because they offend you, my God,
who are all good and deserving of all my love.
I firmly resolve with the help of your grace
to sin no more and to avoid the near occasion of sin.
Amen.

The Act of Contrition is a prayer through which we express sorrow for our failings and for having offended God, and we resolve to change our lives and avoid repeating our mistakes. This prayer is said following the confession of sins during celebration of the sacrament of Reconciliation. It is also a most fitting prayer to end one's day, particularly if you practice the examen.

Peace at the Last

> May he support us all the day long,
> till the shadows lengthen
> and the evening comes
> and the busy world is hushed
> and the fever of life is over
> and our work is done
> —then in his mercy,
> may he give us a safe lodging
> and a holy rest
> and peace at the last.

This beautiful prayer is attributed to John Henry Newman, a nineteenth-century British cardinal and theologian. The prayer is appropriate at the end of a day, as we face the darkness of night, contemplate how we have lived the day, and look forward in hope to a peaceful death.

Eternal Rest

> Eternal rest grant unto him [her], O Lord,
> and let perpetual light shine upon him [her];
> may his [her] soul and all the souls

of the faithful departed,
through the mercy of God, rest in peace.
Amen.

Catholics pray for the dead, being ever joined to them in
the Communion of Saints. Night is a good time to recall
loved ones who have died and to pray for them, asking
God to hasten their journey from purgatory to their eternal
rest in heaven. This prayer is adapted from the first two
lines of the opening prayers in the funeral Mass.

Mass Prayers

Confiteor

> I confess to almighty God
> and to you, my brothers and sisters,
> that I have greatly sinned,
> in my thoughts and in my words,
> in what I have done
> and in what I have failed to do,
> through my fault,
> through my fault,
> through my most grievous fault;
> therefore I ask blessed Mary ever-Virgin,
> all the angels and saints,
> and you, my brothers and sisters,
> to pray for me to the Lord our God.

In preparing for the celebration of the Eucharist, we confess our sins and ask forgiveness from God during the Penitential Act. One option for this prayer is the Confiteor. The Confiteor is also recited during the Liturgy of the Hours. It is customary in some places to strike one's breast when saying "through my fault."

Lord, Have Mercy (*Kyrie, Eleison*)

> You were sent to heal the contrite of heart:
> Lord, have mercy. Or: Kyrie, eleison.

You came to call sinners:
Christ, have mercy. Or: Christe, eleison.

You are seated at the right hand of the Father to
    intercede for us:
Lord, have mercy. Or: Kyrie, eleison.

May almighty God have mercy on us,
forgive us our sins,
and bring us to everlasting life.
Amen.

Another common form of the Penitential Act at Mass is the Lord, Have Mercy or *Kyrie, Eleison* prayer.

Gloria

Glory to God in the highest,
and on earth peace to people of good will.
We praise you,
we bless you,
we adore you,
we glorify you,
we give you thanks for your great glory,
Lord God, heavenly King,
O God, almighty Father.

Lord Jesus Christ, Only Begotten Son,
Lord God, Lamb of God, Son of the Father,
you take away the sins of the world,

have mercy on us;
you take away the sins of the world,
receive our prayer;
you are seated at the right hand of the Father,
have mercy on us.

For you alone are the Holy One,
you alone are the Lord,
you alone are the Most High,
Jesus Christ,
with the Holy Spirit,
in the glory of God the Father.
Amen.

This ancient hymn of the gathered Church is sung or recited by the faithful at Mass, united in the Holy Spirit and entreating God the Father and his Son, Christ the Lamb, to hear our prayer of thanksgiving—that is, the Eucharist. The Gloria is said on Sundays outside Advent and Lent, on solemnities and feasts, and at particular celebrations of a more solemn nature, such as weddings celebrated within Mass.

Nicene Creed

I believe in one God,
the Father almighty,
maker of heaven and earth,
of all things visible and invisible.
I believe in one Lord Jesus Christ,

the Only Begotten Son of God,
born of the Father before all ages.
God from God, Light from Light,
true God from true God,
begotten, not made,
consubstantial with the Father;
through him all things were made.
For us men and for our salvation
he came down from heaven,
and by the Holy Spirit
was incarnate of the Virgin Mary,
and became man.
For our sake,
he was crucified under Pontius Pilate,
he suffered death and was buried,
and rose again on the third day
in accordance with the Scriptures.
He ascended into heaven
and is seated at the right hand of the Father.
He will come again in glory
to judge the living and the dead,
and his kingdom will have no end.
I believe in the Holy Spirit, the Lord,
the giver of life,
who proceeds from the Father and the Son,
who with the Father and the Son is adored
and glorified,
who has spoken through the prophets.
I believe in one, holy, catholic,

and apostolic Church.
I confess one Baptism for the forgiveness of sins,
and I look forward to the resurrection of the dead
and the life of the world to come.
Amen.

This profession of faith was first adopted by the Church at the Council of Nicea (in present-day Turkey) in AD 325. It was written at a time when there was conflict in the Church about what to believe. Because leaders of the Church needed to be clear about what Christians believe about the Trinity in particular, the words of this creed were carefully chosen after considerable debate. Catholics stand and recite this creed at Sunday Mass following the readings and homily.

Holy, Holy (*Sanctus*)

Holy, Holy, Holy Lord God of hosts.
Heaven and earth are full of your glory.
Hosanna in the highest.
Blessed is he who comes in the name of the Lord.
Hosanna in the highest.

This acclamation is sung (or recited) at the beginning of the Liturgy of the Eucharist in response to the Preface proclaimed by the priest. With origins in the gospel account of Jesus entering Jerusalem found in Matthew 21:9, the *Sanctus* is sung by the people and the priest together.

Lamb of God (*Agnus Dei*)

> Lamb of God, you take away the sins of the world,
> have mercy on us.
>
> Lamb of God, you take away the sins of the world,
> have mercy on us.
>
> Lamb of God, you take away the sins of the world,
> grant us peace.

Following the Sign of Peace at Mass, the gathered community prepares to receive the Body and Blood of Christ in Holy Communion by singing this brief antiphon, entreating Jesus, the Lamb of God, to grant mercy and peace.

Prayer before Communion

> Lord, I am not worthy
> that you should enter under my roof,
> but only say the word
> and my soul shall be healed.

Just before we receive Communion at Mass, Catholics pray this simple prayer aloud together. Based on the words of the centurion to Jesus in Matthew 8:8, this prayer reminds us of our utter humility before Jesus, the Lamb of God.

Marian Prayers

The Catholic Church acknowledges and honors Mary. We venerate Mary as being truly the Mother of God, the mother of the redeemer, and the mother of the Church.

In our Catholic belief, we regard Mary not as an equal to God but as a human being with great dignity, a dignity greater than any other saint because of the role she played in our redemption as the mother of Jesus. Her submission to God's will made it possible for the second person of the Trinity to become one of us and thus to save us.

When we pray to Mary, we do not adore her. We pray to honor her and to ask for her help. We ask for her assistance as we would ask our earthly mothers'. We ask her to pray for us as we join our prayers to hers.

Hail, Holy Queen

Hail, holy Queen, Mother of Mercy!
Our life, our sweetness, and our hope!
To you do we cry, poor banished
children of Eve; to you do we send
up our sighs, mourning and weeping
in this valley of tears.
Turn, then, most gracious advocate,
your eyes of mercy toward us; and
after this our exile, show unto us the
blessed fruit of your womb, Jesus;
O clement, O loving, O sweet virgin Mary.
Pray for us, O holy Mother of God,
that we may be made worthy of the promises of
  Christ.

This traditional Catholic prayer is also known by its Latin title, *Salve Regina*. It is a hymn to Mary that has been traditionally sung or recited during Compline (Night Prayer) in the Liturgy of the Hours.

The hymn dates back to the twelfth century. The prayer acknowledges Mary as Queen of Heaven and as a merciful mother who has great compassion for us. In this prayer of petition, we admit our weaknesses and troubles, and we ask Mary to pray on our behalf and to lead us to her son, Jesus. The Hail, Holy Queen is sometimes prayed at the end of the Rosary.

Magnificat

My soul proclaims the greatness of the Lord;
my spirit rejoices in God my Savior
for he has looked with favor on his lowly servant.

From this day all generations will call me blessed:
the Almighty has done great things for me
and holy is his Name.

He has mercy on those who fear him
in every generation.

He has shown the strength of his arm,
and has scattered the proud in their conceit.

He has cast down the mighty from their thrones,
and has lifted up the lowly.

He has filled the hungry with good things,
and the rich he has sent away empty.

He has come to the help of his servant Israel
for he has remembered his promise of mercy,
the promise he made to our fathers,
to Abraham and his children forever.

Glory to the Father, and to the Son,
and to the Holy Spirit:
As it was in the beginning, is now,
and will be forever.

Amen.

This prayer is also known as the Canticle of Mary, and it is one of the most ancient hymns of the Church. The title comes from the first line of the prayer in Latin: *"Magnificat anima mea, Dominum,"* which means, "My soul proclaims the greatness of the Lord."

The Magnificat is Mary's song of praise to God, which is recorded for us in Luke's gospel (1:46–55). When the angel Gabriel visited Mary to announce that God had chosen her to be the mother of his Son, he also told Mary that her cousin Elizabeth was expecting. Mary went to visit Elizabeth, who lived in Judah. Luke tells us that when Mary greeted her cousin, the baby leaped in Elizabeth's womb, and Elizabeth, moved by the Holy Spirit, responded with what has become part of the Hail Mary: "Most blessed are you among women, and blessed is the fruit of your womb" (Luke 1:42). Mary then rejoiced with Elizabeth by proclaiming the greatness of the

Lord in an expression of faith that would become known as the Canticle of Mary or the Magnificat.

This prayer is a song of praise for the favors God bestowed on Mary, for the kindnesses shown toward Israel, and for the fulfillment of the promises made to Abraham and his descendants.

Today this prayer is sung or recited each day in the Liturgy of the Hours during Vespers (Evening Prayer).

Memorare

Remember, O most gracious Virgin Mary,
that never was it known
that anyone who fled to your protection,
implored your help,
or sought your intercession
was left unaided.
Inspired by this confidence,
we fly unto you, O Virgin of Virgins our mother;
to you do we come, before you we stand,
sinful and sorrowful;
O Mother of the Word Incarnate,
despise not our petitions,
but in your mercy hear and answer us.
Amen.

The word *memorare* is a Latin term that means "remember." This is another traditional and popular prayer to Mary. Like the Hail, Holy Queen, this too is a prayer that is several centuries old. In this prayer we ask Mary, our mother, to intercede for us.

Catholics believe that Mary and the saints are our allies in heaven. When we pray to Mary, we ask her to intercede for us with her Son.

Regina Coeli (Queen of Heaven)

V. Queen of Heaven, rejoice, alleluia,
R. For he whom you did merit to bear, alleluia,

V. Has risen, as he said, alleluia.
R. Pray for us to God, alleluia.

V. Rejoice and be glad, O Virgin Mary, alleluia!
R. For the Lord has truly risen, alleluia.

O God,
who gave joy to the world
through the Resurrection of your Son,
our Lord Jesus Christ, grant, we beseech you,
that through the intercession of the Virgin Mary,
his Mother, we may obtain the joys of everlasting life.
Through the same Christ our Lord. Amen.

Regina Coeli is a Latin phrase that means "Queen of Heaven." It is recited or sung during Compline (Night Prayer), the last hour of the Liturgy of the Hours, during certain times of the year. The Regina Coeli is said in place of the Angelus (see pages 117–118) during the Easter season. It is often prayed while standing.

The origin of this prayer is not clear, and the author is not known. It is generally estimated that the practice of reciting or singing this prayer dates back to the twelfth century.

Praying with the Saints

In the Catholic Church the word *saint* is used in two ways. On the one hand, we speak about the saints as those individuals who have died and who have been recognized by the Church as models of holiness and thus officially declared or canonized saints. On the other hand, we also believe that all members of the Church—those who are still pilgrims on earth, those who have died and are waiting for purification in purgatory, and those who are in heaven—are all members of what we call the Communion of Saints.

In this section of the book, we share with you prayers passed on to us by some of our most beloved saints. These are persons whom the Church, through the process of canonization, has declared saints. Honoring the saints in heaven by praying for their intercession is a tradition that dates back to the early centuries of the Church. We regard the saints as members of our spiritual family to whom we can turn for help through prayer. Just as we ask each other and our friends to pray for us, we ask the saints to intercede for us, with the understanding that the Father will grant us what is best for us.

We find comfort in their words because their prayers are timeless. They reflect the same universal struggles that we encounter today.

You will also find prayers from recent popes, including Pope Francis and Pope emeritus Benedict XVI.

St. Augustine (AD 354–430)

Augustine was a respected philosopher, theologian, and defender of the faith. He was bishop of Hippo, a city located in modern-day Algeria. Augustine is considered a saint both by Catholics and Anglicans. We celebrate his feast day on August 28.

Prayer to the Holy Spirit

Breathe in me, O Holy Spirit,
that my thoughts may all be holy.
Act in me, O Holy Spirit,
that my work, too, may be holy.
Draw my heart, O Holy Spirit,
that I love but what is holy.
Strengthen me, O Holy Spirit,
to defend all that is holy.
Guard me, then, O Holy Spirit,
that I always may be holy.
Amen.

Prayer for Difficult Times

God of our life,
there are days when the burdens we carry
chafe our shoulders and weigh us down;
when the road seems dreary and endless,
the skies gray and threatening;
when our lives have no music in them,
and our hearts are lonely,
and our souls have lost their courage.

Flood the path with light,
turn our eyes to where the skies are full
of promise;
tune our hearts to brave music;
give us the sense of comradeship
with heroes and saints of every age;
and so quicken our spirits
that we may be able to encourage
the souls of all who journey with us
on the road of life,
to your honor and glory.
Amen.

St. Patrick (Fifth Century)

Although the exact dates of his life are uncertain, most historians agree that during the fifth century Patrick was active as a missionary and later became a bishop in Ireland. He is the patron saint of that country, and as we're sure you know, we celebrate his feast day on March 17.

St. Patrick's Breastplate

I arise today through God's strength to pilot me,
God's might to uphold me,
God's wisdom to guide me,
God's eye to see before me,
Gods ear to hear me, God's word to speak for me,
God's hand to guard me,
God's way to lie before me,

God's shield to protect me,
God's host to secure me—
against snares of devils,
against temptations and vices,
against inclinations of nature,
against everyone who shall wish me ill,
afar and anear, alone and in a crowd.

Christ, be with me, Christ before me,
Christ behind me,
Christ in me, Christ beneath me, Christ above me,
Christ on my right, Christ on my left,
Christ where I lie, Christ where I sit,
Christ where I arise, Christ in the heart
of everyone who thinks of me,
Christ in the mouth of every man
who speaks of me,
Christ in every eye that sees me,
Christ in every ear that hears me.
Salvation is of the Lord.
Salvation is of the Lord.
Salvation is of the Christ.
May your salvation, O Lord, be ever with us.

There are various adaptations of this prayer, and the above
is an abbreviated version of it.

St. Francis of Assisi (1182–1226)

Francis was born into a wealthy family in Assisi, Italy, in 1182. At an early age, he renounced his family's wealth and went to live among and serve the poor and to preach the Gospel on street corners. Although he was never ordained a priest, he founded the Franciscan Order and is one of the most venerated saints in history. It is this saint's name that Pope Francis took when he was elected to the papacy in March 2013. We celebrate St. Francis's feast day on October 4.

Peace Prayer

Lord, make me an instrument of your peace;
where there is hatred, let me sow love;
where there is injury, pardon;
where there is error, truth;
where there is doubt, faith;
where there is despair, hope;
where there is darkness, light;
and where there is sadness, joy.

O Divine Master,
grant that I may not so much seek
to be consoled, as to console;
to be understood, as to understand;
to be loved as to love.

For it is in giving that we receive;
it is in pardoning that we are pardoned;

and it is in dying that we are born to eternal life.
Amen.

Canticle of Brother Sun

Most High, all-powerful, good Lord,
yours are the praises, the glory, the honor,
and all blessing.
To you alone, Most High, do they belong,
and no man is worthy to mention your name.
Be praised, my Lord, through all your creatures,
especially through my lord Brother Sun,
who brings the day;
and you give light through him.
And he is beautiful and radiant in all his splendor!
Of you, Most High, he bears the likeness.
Praise be you, my Lord, through Sister Moon
and the stars; in heaven you formed them
clear and precious and beautiful.
Praised be you, my Lord, through Brother Wind,
and through the air, cloudy and serene,
and every kind of weather through which
you give sustenance to your creatures.
Praised be you, my Lord, through Sister Water,
which is very useful and humble
and precious and chaste.
Praised be you, my Lord, through Brother Fire,
through whom you light the night;
and he is beautiful
and playful and robust and strong.

Praised be you, my Lord,
through Sister Mother Earth,
who sustains us and governs us
and who produces varied fruits
with colored flowers and herbs.
Praised be you, my Lord,
through those who give pardon for your love,
and bear infirmity and tribulation.
Blessed are those who endure in peace,
for by you, Most High, they shall be crowned.
Praised be you, my Lord,
through our Sister Bodily Death,
from whom no living person can escape.
Woe to those who die in mortal sin.
Blessed are those whom death will find
in your most holy will,
for the second death shall do them no harm.
Praise and bless my Lord,
and give him thanks
and serve him with great humility.
Amen.

The Canticle of Brother Sun is also a popular prayer by this beloved saint. This is a prayer of praise to God for his creation. The phrase "praise be to you" (*laudato si* in Latin), which is repeated in most verses of this prayer, was chosen by Pope Francis to be the title of his 2015 encyclical letter on the Christian duty to care for the environment.

St. Ignatius of Loyola (1491–1556)

Ignatius was a Spanish knight of Basque heritage who lived in the first half of the sixteenth century. After being seriously wounded in battle, he had a vision that led him to a secluded life of prayer and devotion. He became a leading voice of the Counter-Reformation and the founder of the Society of Jesus, popularly known as the Jesuits. We celebrate his feast day on July 31.

The Prayer for Generosity and the Prayer of Offering were written by St. Ignatius. While it is unlikely that Ignatius composed the Anima Christi, it was so popular during his lifetime that he placed the prayer at the beginning of his Spiritual Exercises. The Spiritual Exercises are a series of meditations and prayers written by St. Ignatius for those making a thirty-day retreat.

Anima Christi

Soul of Christ, sanctify me;
Body of Christ, save me;
Blood of Christ, inebriate me;
Water from the side of Christ, wash me;
Passion of Christ, strengthen me;
O good Jesus, hear me;
Within your wounds hide me;
Separated from you, let me never be;
From the evil one protect me;
At the hour of my death, call me;
And close to you bid me;
That with your saints, I may be,

Praising you forever and ever.
Amen.

Prayer for Generosity

Lord, teach me to be generous,
to serve you as you deserve,
to give and not to count the cost,
to fight and not to heed the wounds,
to toil and not to seek for rest,
to labor and not to look for any reward,
save that of knowing that I do your holy will.
Amen.

Prayer of Offering (*Suscipe*)

Receive, O Lord, all my liberty.
Take my memory, my understanding,
and my entire will.
Whatsoever I have or hold, you have given me;
I give it all back to you and surrender it
wholly to be governed by your will.
Give me only your love and your grace;
with these I will be rich enough,
and ask for nothing more.

Mary, Queen of Scots (1542–1587)

Mary Stuart, Queen of Scots, is not a canonized saint;
yet Catholics continue to venerate her. As queen, she
attempted to restore the Catholic Church in England. In
attempting to overthrow Queen Elizabeth I, she lost her
life. She was executed in 1587.

Prayer for a Magnanimous Heart

O God, keep us from all pettiness:
Let us be large in thought, in word and deed.
Let us be done with fault finding and
leave off all self-seeking.
May we put away all pretense and
meet each other face-to-face
without self-pity and without prejudice.
May we never be hasty in judgment
and always generous.
Let us always take time for all things,
and make us grow calm, serene, and gentle.
Teach us to put into action our better impulses,
to be straightforward and unafraid.
Grant that we may realize that it is the
little things that create differences,
that in the big things of life we are as one.
And, O Lord God, let us not forget to be kind.

Blessed John Henry Newman (1801–1890)

John Henry Newman was a Catholic cardinal and theologian who wielded great influence in nineteenth-century England. He grew up as a member of the Church of England and was ordained as an Anglican priest. In 1845 Newman left the Church of England, together with some of his followers, to become Catholic. In 1879, shortly after he was ordained a Catholic priest, he was made a cardinal and was based in Birmingham, England. Newman was declared "Blessed," a step toward becoming a

saint, in 2010 by Pope Benedict XVI. His feast day is celebrated in the Church's liturgical calendar on January 5.

The Pillar of the Cloud

Lead, kindly Light, amid the encircling gloom,
Lead thou me on!
The night is dark, and I am far from home,
Lead thou me on!
Keep thou my feet! I do not ask to see
The distant scene—one step enough for me.

I was not ever thus, nor prayed that thou
Shouldst lead me on;
I loved to choose and see my path; but now
Lead thou me on!
I loved the garish day, and, spite of fears,
Pride ruled my will: remember not past years!

So long thy power hath blest me, sure it still
Will lead me on,
O'er moor and fen, o'er crag and torrent, till
The night is gone,
And with the morn those angel faces smile
Which I have loved long since, and lost awhile.

Pope Leo XIII (1810–1903)

Often known as the "Rosary Pope" because of his devotion to the Blessed Virgin, Pope Leo's pontificate lasted
from 1878 until his death in 1903. His was the third

longest pontificate in history. Leo XIII was revered as an
intellectual and is widely known for his development
of Catholic social teaching, particularly his watershed
encyclical *Rerum Novarum* (*Of Revolutionary Change: Rights
and Duties of Capital and Labor*).

Prayer to St. Joseph

To you, O blessed Joseph,
do we come in our tribulation,
and having implored the help
of your most holy Spouse,
we confidently invoke your patronage also.

Through that charity which bound you
to the Immaculate Virgin Mother of God
and through the paternal love
with which you embraced the Child Jesus,
we humbly beg you graciously
to regard the inheritance
which Jesus Christ has purchased by his Blood,
and with your power and strength
to aid us in our necessities.

O most watchful guardian of the Holy Family,
defend the chosen children of Jesus Christ;
O most loving father, ward off from us
every contagion of error and corrupting influence;
O our most mighty protector, be kind to us
and from heaven assist us in our struggle
with the power of darkness.

As once you rescued the Child Jesus
from deadly peril,
so now protect God's Holy Church
from the snares of the enemy
and from all adversity;
shield, too, each one of us
by your constant protection,
so that, supported by your example and your aid,
we may be able to live piously, to die in holiness,
and to obtain eternal happiness in heaven.
Amen.

St. Padre Pio (1887–1968)

Francesco Forgione (later known as Padre Pio) was born
in Pietrelcina, Italy, a small farming town. He became a
member of the Capuchin Order of the Friars Minor and
was ordained a priest in 1910. A deeply spiritual man
with great devotion to the Rosary, Padre Pio struggled
with poor health all his life. In his monastery at San
Giovanni Rotondo, he lived a simple life as a Franciscan
and brought many people back to the faith. He died at
the age of eighty-one in September 1968. We celebrate his
feast day on September 23.

A Prayer for Trust and Confidence in God's Mercy
O Lord, we ask for a boundless confidence
and trust in your divine mercy,
and the courage to accept

the crosses and sufferings
which bring immense goodness
to our souls and that of your Church.
Help us to love you
with a pure and contrite heart,
and to humble ourselves beneath your Cross,
as we climb the mountain of holiness,
carrying our cross that leads to heavenly glory.
May we receive you
with great faith and love in Holy Communion,
and allow you to act in us as you desire
for your greater glory.
O Jesus, most adorable Heart
and eternal fountain of Divine Love,
may our prayer find favor
before the Divine Majesty
of Your heavenly Father.
Amen.

St. Teresa of Calcutta (1910–1997)

Known throughout the world simply as Mother Teresa, St.
Teresa of Calcutta was born in Skopje, Macedonia, in 1910.
As a Catholic nun, she founded the Missionaries of Charity,
whose mission is to care for the poorest of the poor around
the world. Mother Teresa received the Nobel Peace Prize
for her humanitarian work in 1979 and was given the title
"Blessed" in 2003. She was canonized by Pope Francis on
September 4, 2016. Her feast day is September 5.

Prayer for Our Family

Heavenly Father,
you have given us a model of life
in the Holy Family of Nazareth.
Help us, O Loving Father,
to make our family another Nazareth
where love, peace, and joy reign.
May it be deeply contemplative,
intensely eucharistic, and vibrant with joy.

Help us to stay together
in joy and sorrow through family prayer.
Teach us to see Jesus
in the members of our family,
especially in their distressing disguise.
May the eucharistic heart of Jesus
make our hearts meek and humble like his
and help us to carry out our family duties
in a holy way.

May we love one another
as God loves each one of us,
more and more each day,
and forgive each other's faults
as you forgive our sins.
Help us, O loving Father,
to take whatever you give
and give whatever you take with a big smile.

Immaculate Heart of Mary,
cause of our joy, pray for us.
St. Joseph, pray for us.
Holy Guardian Angels,
be always with us;
guide and protect us. Amen.

Radiating Christ

Dear Jesus, help us to spread your fragrance
everywhere we go.
Flood our souls with your spirit and life.
Penetrate and possess our whole being so utterly
that all our lives may only be a radiance of yours.
Shine through us and be so in us that every soul
we come in contact with
may feel your presence in our souls.
Let them look up and see no longer us but only
    Jesus!
Stay with us and then we shall begin to shine as
    you shine, so to be a light to others.
Let us preach you without preaching,
not by words but by example,
    by the catching force,
the sympathetic influence of what we do,
the evident fullness of the love our hearts bear
for you.
Amen.

This is an adaptation by Mother Teresa of a prayer written
by Blessed John Henry Newman.

Thomas Merton (1915–1968)

Thomas Merton was a Catholic writer who became a Trappist monk at the Abbey of Gethsemani in Kentucky. He was ordained a priest in 1949 and took the name Fr. Louis. One of the twentieth century's most important thinkers, Merton wrote more than sixty books, among them his autobiography, *The Seven Storey Mountain*, which became one of the most influential religious books of that century.

The Road Ahead

My Lord God,
I have no idea where I am going.
I do not see the road ahead of me.
I cannot know for certain where it will end.
Nor do I really know myself,
and the fact that I think I am following your will
does not mean that I am actually doing so.
But I believe that the desire to please you
does in fact please you.
And I hope I have that desire
in all that I am doing.
I hope that I will never do anything
apart from that desire.
And I know that if I do this,
you will lead me on the right road
though I may know nothing about it.
Therefore will I trust you always
Though I may seem to be lost
and in the shadow of death.

I will not fear, for you are ever with me,
and you will never leave me
to face my struggles alone.
Amen.

St. John Paul II (1920–2005)

Born as Karol Jozef Wojtyla, St. John Paul II was born in Poland, the youngest of three children. After attending seminary in Krakow, he was ordained a priest in 1946 and was appointed auxiliary bishop of Krakow in 1958. In October 1962, Bishop Wojtyla participated in the Second Vatican Council. He was appointed archbishop of Krakow in 1964, and in 1967 he was promoted to the College of Cardinals. In 1978 Karol Jozef Wojtyla was elected pope, and he chose the name John Paul II. He has left many writings that guide the Church today, among them the *Catechism of the Catholic Church*. John Paul II was declared a saint on April 27, 2014. We celebrate his feast day on October 22.

Prayer for Everlasting Peace

To the Creator of nature and man,
of truth and beauty, I pray:
Hear my voice, for it is the voice of the victims
of all wars and violence
among individuals and nations.
Hear my voice, for it is the voice of all children
who suffer and will suffer
when people put their faith in weapons and war.
Hear my voice when I beg you to instill

into the hearts of all human beings
the wisdom of peace, the strength of justice,
and the joy of fellowship.
Hear my voice, for I speak for the multitudes
in every country
and in every period of history
who do not want war
and are ready to walk the road of peace.
Hear my voice and grant insight and strength
so that we may always respond to hatred
with love,
to injustice with total dedication to justice,
to need with the sharing of self,
to war with peace.
O God, hear my voice and grant unto the world
your everlasting peace.

Pope Benedict XVI (Born 1927)

Joseph Aloisius Ratzinger was born in 1927 in Bavaria, Germany. He and his brother entered the seminary in 1945, and both were ordained priests in 1951. Joseph became a professor at the University of Bonn in 1959 and participated in the Second Vatican Council as a theological consultant.

In 1977 he was appointed archbishop of Munich and Freising, and in 1981 Pope John Paul II appointed him to be the head of the Sacred Congregation for the Doctrine of the Faith. He was elected pope in 2005, and he assumed the name Benedict XVI. Benedict XVI followed in the footsteps of his predecessor in defending traditional Catholic doctrine and values. On February 11, 2013, Pope Benedict announced his resignation as pope because of his advanced age, and he continues to reside in the Vatican while living a private life as Pope emeritus.

Prayer to Mary to Learn to Love

Holy Mary, Mother of God,
you have given the world its true light,
Jesus, your Son—the Son of God.
You abandoned yourself completely
to God's call
and thus became a wellspring
of the goodness which flows forth from him.
Show us Jesus. Lead us to him.
Teach us to know and love him,
so that we too can become capable of true love
and be fountains of living water
in the midst of a thirsting world.
Amen.

—*Deus Caritas Est* (*God Is Love*), #42

Pope Francis (Born 1936)

Born Jorge Mario Bergoglio in Buenos Aires, Argentina, Pope Francis was the first Jesuit to be elected pope. He worked for a short time as a chemical technologist and nightclub bouncer in his youth before entering seminary training. Jorge was ordained to the priesthood as a Jesuit in 1969. He became archbishop of Buenos Aires in 1998 and was made a cardinal by Pope John Paul II in 2001. In the papal conclave of March 2013, he was elected pope, succeeding Pope Benedict XVI, and took the name Francis.

Pope Francis's deep devotion to Mary, Undoer of Knots, had a great impact on his spiritual life. While studying in Germany in the 1980s, he discovered this devotion at a church in Augsburg. There Francis first saw a painting of Mary under this title. She is surrounded by angels, standing on the crescent moon and crushing the head of a serpent (Satan). Mary is untying one of several large knots in a ribbon she holds. While the origins of the image are not certain, some scholars speculate that inspiration for the image comes from St. Irenaeus's description of Mary having loosed the knot of Eve's sin by her obedience to the will of God. The prayer below has the Imprimatur of then-Archbishop Jorge Bergoglio of Buenos Aires.

Prayer to Mary, Undoer of Knots

Holy Mary,
full of the presence of God,
during the days of your earthly life
you accepted in all humility the will of the Father,
and the Evil One was never able to ensnare you
with his confusion.

Already together with your Son you interceded
for our difficulties
and with all simplicity and patience
you gave us the example of how to disentangle
the tangles of our lives.

And remaining always as our mother,
you arrange and reveal to us
the bonds that unite us with the Lord.

Holy Mary, Mother of God and our mother,
you who with a maternal heart untie the knots
that constrict our lives,
we ask you to receive into your hands [name],
and free us from the bonds and confusions
with which our enemy torments us.

By your grace, by your intercession,
with your example free us from all evil,
our Lady, and untie the knots
that prevent us from being united with God
so that, free from all confusion and error,
we may encounter him in all things,
rest our hearts in him,
and serve him always in our brothers and sisters.
Amen.

Prayer to the Holy Family

Jesus, Mary, and Joseph,
in you we contemplate
the splendor of true love;
to you we turn with trust.

Holy Family of Nazareth,
grant that our families too

may be places of communion and prayer,
authentic schools of the Gospel
and small domestic churches.

Holy Family of Nazareth,
may families never again experience
violence, rejection, and division;
may all who have been hurt or scandalized
find ready comfort and healing.

Holy Family of Nazareth,
make us once more mindful
of the sacredness and inviolability of the family,
and its beauty in God's plan.

Jesus, Mary, and Joseph,
graciously hear our prayer.
Amen.

—*Amoris Laetitia (The Joy of Love)*, #325

Part 3

Devotions

In our home we have a thirteen-inch statue of the Sacred Heart of Jesus. This image of God's mercy has been a permanent fixture in my (John's) family all my life. The statue was a gift from my uncle to my grandparents, who consecrated their family to the Sacred Heart of Jesus. When I was growing up, the image had a prominent place in the kitchen of our home. The Sacred Heart was there when we celebrated anniversaries, birthdays, and special events. It was there when we were saddened by my mother's illness and as we cried at her dying. It remained there when my father remarried, and the Sacred Heart statue went with him to the nursing home during his last days. When my father passed away, my sister gave the Sacred Heart statue to Teri and me.

I remember praying in front of this statue as a boy with my whole family in the evenings of late October. After dinner, all of us—my grandparents, parents, brother, sister, and I—would gather in the kitchen to pray the Rosary facing the statue. My memories of those evenings are rich with sounds, images, and lingering aromas. I can still hear the voices of my family members reciting the Hail Mary, can see their faces and the postures of their bodies in prayer, and can almost smell the aroma and hear the crackling of roasting chestnuts on the stove—a wonderful snack we shared after the Rosary.

These memories of family prayer have become part of who I am. There is something nostalgic about family prayer traditions. When we ask engaged couples with whom we work to share memories of family prayer times, their voices soften as they tell their stories. These are precious moments in the lives of the faithful.

Devotional prayer anchors particularly deep in our souls. Perhaps it is the ritual actions, repetitive words, and communal nature of this type of prayer. But something deeply formative is offered to us in the Church's devotions. They shape our identity as Catholics and, along with the liturgy and personal prayer, become for us the glue of the spiritual life. The Church has many devotions; here we introduce, or reacquaint you with, eight that are quite common.

The Rosary

The Rosary is a prayer of meditation on the mysteries of God's salvation. Recalling God's love for us as expressed through the lives of Jesus and Mary, the four sets of mysteries each include five decades, comprised of an Our Father, ten Hail Marys, and a Glory Be. Each set of mysteries is prayed according to the day of the week:

- Monday: the Joyful Mysteries

- Tuesday: the Sorrowful Mysteries

- Wednesday: the Glorious Mysteries

- Thursday: the Luminous Mysteries

- Friday: the Sorrowful Mysteries

- Saturday: the Joyful Mysteries

- Sunday: the Glorious Mysteries

According to legend, St. Dominic received the idea of the Rosary from Mary during an apparition in 1214, but the tradition of praying fifty or 150 Hail Marys seemed to exist before St. Dominic. However, the spread of this devotion was due in large part to the Order of Preachers, commonly known as Dominicans, who were founded by Dominic. The Rosary was officially recognized as a Catholic devotion in 1569 by Pope Pius V.

The practice of saying the Rosary with three sets of mysteries—Joyful, Sorrowful, and Glorious—remained unchanged until the twentieth-first century. In 2002 Pope John Paul II introduced a fourth set known as the Luminous Mysteries.

Many people use rosary beads when praying the Rosary, but they are not essential. The ten fingers of one's hand are just as useful.

How to Pray the Rosary

A dear priest and former pastor wrote a booklet for his parishioners on how to pray the Rosary. With his permission, we adapt below the directions he gave us on praying the Rosary.

1. Begin by making the Sign of the Cross (page 33), holding the crucifix.

2. While holding the crucifix, recite the Apostles' Creed (page 36–37).

3. On the first large bead, say one Our Father (page 34), followed by three Hail Marys (page 35) on the three smaller beads.

4. Then pray one Glory Be (page 33–34). No bead is designated for the Glory Be.

5. Identify the first mystery that you are meditating on, and then pray one Our Father on the large bead of the rosary.

6. Pray ten Hail Marys, counting them on the small beads of the rosary, followed by a Glory Be.

7. At the end of the Rosary, pray the Hail, Holy Queen (page 55).

The pages that follow provide the four groups of mysteries and their biblical references.

The Joyful Mysteries

1. The Annunciation

"The angel Gabriel was sent from God to a town of Galilee called Nazareth, to a virgin betrothed to a man named Joseph, of the house of David, and the virgin's name was Mary. And coming to her, he said, 'Hail, favored one! The Lord is with you.' . . . Then the angel said to her, 'Do not be afraid, Mary, for you have found favor with God. Behold, you will conceive in your womb and bear a son, and you shall name him Jesus. . . .' Mary said, 'Behold, I am the handmaid of the Lord. May it be done to me according to your word'" (Luke 1:26–28, 30–31, 38).

2. The Visitation

"During those days Mary set out and traveled to the hill country in haste to a town of Judah, where she entered the house of Zechariah and greeted Elizabeth. When

Elizabeth heard Mary's greeting, the infant leaped in her womb, and Elizabeth, filled with the holy Spirit, cried out in a loud voice and said, 'Most blessed are you among women, and blessed is the fruit of your womb. . . . Blessed are you who believed that what was spoken to you by the Lord would be fulfilled'" (Luke 1:39–42, 45).

3. The Birth of Jesus (The Nativity)

"In those days a decree went out from Caesar Augustus that the whole world should be enrolled. . . . And Joseph too went up from Galilee from the town of Nazareth to Judea, to the city of David that is called Bethlehem, because he was of the house and family of David, to be enrolled with Mary, his betrothed, who was with child. While they were there, the time came for her to have her child, and she gave birth to her firstborn son. She wrapped him in swaddling clothes and laid him in a manger, because there was no room for them in the inn" (Luke 2:1, 4–7).

4. The Presentation in the Temple

"When the days were completed for their purification according to the law of Moses, they took him up to Jerusalem to present him to the Lord. . . . Now there was a man in Jerusalem whose name was Simeon. . . . It had been revealed to him by the holy Spirit that he should not see death before he had seen the Messiah of the Lord. He came in the Spirit into the temple; and when the parents brought in the child Jesus to perform the custom of the law in regard to him, he took him into his arms and blessed God, saying: 'Now, Master, you may let your servant go in peace, according to your word, for my eyes have seen your salvation, which you prepared in sight of all the peoples'" (Luke 2:22, 25–31).

5. The Finding of Jesus in the Temple

"Each year his parents went to Jerusalem for the feast of Passover, and when he was twelve years old, they went up according to festival custom. After they had completed its days, as they were returning, the boy Jesus remained behind in Jerusalem, but his parents did not know it. Thinking that he was in the caravan, they journeyed for a day and looked for him among their relatives and acquaintances, but not finding him, they returned to Jerusalem to look for him. After three days they found him in the temple, sitting in the midst of the teachers, listening to them and asking them questions . . . and his mother said to him, 'Son, why have you done this to us? Your father and I have been looking for you with great anxiety.' And he said to them, 'Why were you looking for me? Did you not know that I must be in my Father's house?' But they did not understand what he said to them" (Luke 2:41–46, 48–50).

The Luminous Mysteries

1. The Baptism of Jesus in the Jordan

"Then Jesus came from Galilee to John at the Jordan to be baptized by him. John tried to prevent him, saying, 'I need to be baptized by you, and yet you are coming to me?' Jesus said to him in reply, 'Allow it now, for thus it is fitting for us to fulfill all righteousness.' Then he allowed him. After Jesus was baptized, he came up from the water and behold, the heavens were opened [for him], and he saw the Spirit of God descending like a dove [and] coming upon him. And a voice came from the heavens, saying, 'This is my beloved Son, with whom I am well pleased'" (Matthew 3:13–17).

2. The Wedding at Cana

"On the third day there was a wedding in Cana in Galilee, and the mother of Jesus was there. Jesus and his disciples were also invited to the wedding. When the wine ran short, the mother of Jesus said to him, 'They have no wine.' [And] Jesus said to her, 'Woman, how does your concern affect me? My hour has not yet come.' His mother said to the servers, 'Do whatever he tells you.' . . . Jesus told them, 'Fill the jars with water.' So they filled them to the brim. Then he told them, 'Draw some out now and take it to the headwaiter.' So they took it. And when the headwaiter tasted the water that had become wine, . . . the headwaiter called the bridegroom and said to him, 'Everyone serves good wine first, and then when people have drunk freely, an inferior one; but you have kept the good wine until now.' Jesus did this as the beginning of his signs in Cana in Galilee and so revealed his glory, and his disciples began to believe in him" (John 2:1–5, 7–11).

3. The Proclamation of the Kingdom of God

"Jesus came to Galilee proclaiming the gospel of God: 'This is the time of fulfillment. The kingdom of God is at hand. Repent, and believe in the gospel.'

As he passed by the Sea of Galilee, he saw Simon and his brother Andrew. . . . Jesus said to them, 'Come after me, and I will make you fishers of men.' Then they abandoned their nets and followed him. . . . Then they came to Capernaum, and on the Sabbath he entered the synagogue and taught. The people were astonished at his teaching, for he taught them as one having authority and not as the scribes" (Mark 1:14–18, 21–22).

4. The Transfiguration

"He took Peter, John, and James and went up the mountain to pray. While he was praying his face changed in appearance and his clothing became dazzling white. And behold, two men were conversing with him, Moses and Elijah. . . . Peter and his companions had been overcome by sleep, but becoming fully awake, they saw his glory and the two men standing with him. . . . A cloud came and cast a shadow over them, and they became frightened when they entered the cloud. Then from the cloud came a voice that said, 'This is my chosen Son; listen to him'" (Luke 9:28–30, 32, 34–35).

5. The Eucharist

"While they were eating, Jesus took bread, said the blessing, broke it, and giving it to his disciples said, 'Take and eat; this is my body.' Then he took a cup, gave thanks, and gave it to them, saying, 'Drink from it, all of you, for this is my blood of the covenant, which will be shed on behalf of many for the forgiveness of sins'" (Matthew 26:26–28).

The Sorrowful Mysteries

1. The Agony in the Garden

"Then Jesus came with them to a place called Gethsemane, and he said to his disciples, 'Sit here while I go over there and pray.' He took along Peter and the two sons of Zebedee, and began to feel sorrow and distress. Then he said to them, 'My soul is sorrowful even to death. Remain here and keep watch with me.' He advanced a little and fell prostrate in prayer, saying, 'My Father, if it is possible, let this cup pass from me; yet, not as I will, but as you will'" (Matthew 26:36–39).

2. The Scourging at the Pillar

"They bound Jesus, led him away, and handed him over to Pilate. Pilate questioned him, 'Are you the king of the Jews?' He said to him in reply, 'You say so'" (Mark 15:1b–2). "Then Pilate took Jesus and had him scourged" (John 19:1). "They blindfolded him and questioned him, saying, 'Prophesy! Who is it that struck you?'" (Luke 22:64). "So Pilate, wishing to satisfy the crowd, released Barabbas to them and, after he had Jesus scourged, handed him over to be crucified" (Mark 15:15).

3. The Crowning with Thorns

"The soldiers led him away inside the palace, that is, the praetorium. . . . They clothed him in purple and, weaving a crown of thorns, placed it on him. They began to salute him with, 'Hail, King of the Jews!' and kept striking his head with a reed and spitting upon him. They knelt before him in homage. And when they had mocked him, they stripped him of the purple cloak, dressed him in his own clothes, and led him out to crucify him" (Mark 15:16–20).

4. The Carrying of the Cross

"As they were going out, they met a Cyrenian named Simon; this man they pressed into service to carry his cross" (Matthew 27:32–32). "A large crowd of people followed Jesus, including many women who mourned and lamented him. Jesus turned to them and said, 'Daughters of Jerusalem, do not weep for me; weep instead for yourselves and for your children'" (Luke 23:27–28).

5. The Crucifixion and Death

"When they came to the place called the Skull, they crucified him and the criminals there, one on his right, the other on his left. [Then Jesus said, 'Father, forgive them, they know not what they do.'] They divided his garments by casting lots. The people stood by and watched; the rulers, meanwhile, sneered at him and said, 'He saved others, let him save himself if he is the chosen one, the Messiah of God.' . . . Jesus cried out in a loud voice, 'Father, into your hands I commend my spirit'; and when he had said this he breathed his last. The centurion who witnessed what had happened glorified God and said, 'This man was innocent beyond doubt'" (Luke 23:33–35, 46–47).

The Glorious Mysteries

1. The Resurrection

"After the sabbath, as the first day of the week was dawning, Mary Magdalene and the other Mary came to see the tomb. And behold, there was a great earthquake; for an angel of the Lord descended from heaven, approached, rolled back the stone, and sat upon it. His appearance was like lightning and his clothing was white as snow. The guards were shaken with fear of him and became like dead men. Then the angel said to the women in reply, 'Do not be afraid! I know that you are seeking Jesus the crucified. He is not here, for he has been raised just as he said. Come and see the place where he lay'" (Matthew 28:1–6).

2. The Ascension

"Then he led them [out] as far as Bethany, raised his hands, and blessed them. As he blessed them he parted from them and was taken up to heaven. They did him homage and then returned to Jerusalem with great joy, and they were continually in the temple praising God" (Luke 24:50–53).

3. The Coming of the Holy Spirit

"And I will ask the Father, and he will give you another Advocate to be with you always, the Spirit of truth" (John 14:16–17a). "When the time for Pentecost was fulfilled, they were all in one place together. And suddenly there came from the sky a noise like a strong driving wind, and it filled the entire house in which they were. Then there appeared to them tongues as of fire, which parted and came to rest on each one of them. And they were all filled with the holy Spirit and began to speak in different tongues, as the Spirit enabled them to proclaim" (Acts 2:1–4).

4. The Assumption of Mary to Heaven

"A great sign appeared in the sky, a woman clothed with the sun, with the moon under her feet, and on her head a crown of twelve stars" (Revelation 12:1). "Blessed are you, daughter, by the Most High God, above all the women on earth; and blessed be the Lord God, the creator of heaven and earth" (Judith 13:18).

5. The Coronation of Mary in Heaven

"And Mary said: 'My soul proclaims the greatness of the Lord; my spirit rejoices in God my savior. For he has looked upon his handmaid's lowliness; behold, from now on will all ages call me blessed. The Mighty One has done great things for me, and holy is his name'" (Luke 1:46–49).

The Stations of the Cross

We live in Nashville, Tennessee, a city where Catholics are only a small segment of the population. Earlier this year our friend, who is Catholic and who works as the director of daycare at a Methodist church, said to us with a sense of surprise, "The pastor at the church where I work is excited about adding the Stations of the Cross to their Lenten practices this year." She was pleased to know that this traditional Catholic devotion was being appreciated and embraced by other Christians.

The Stations of the Cross—or Way of the Cross, as it is sometimes called—is a devotion that goes back to the early centuries of the Church, when pilgrims to Jerusalem would trace the final journey of Jesus during his Passion. Today that path is called the Via Dolorosa (Way of Suffering). John and I made a pilgrimage to the Holy Land with members of our parish, and were able to pray the Stations along the Via Dolorosa in Jerusalem. As our small group walked from station to station up the narrow road while carrying a large cross, we were flanked by merchants selling their wares. Through the eyes of our faith, we all felt transported back in time and were soberly aware of what Jesus might have experienced.

Praying the Stations of the Cross was common practice across Europe during the twelfth and thirteenth centuries, but during the Reformation, Protestants rejected this devotion because of its link with indulgences, a Catholic tradition they vehemently opposed. Today, many mainline Protestant parishes are returning to this devotion because of its richness in helping us appreciate Christ's Passion, Death, and Resurrection.

The Stations of the Cross

The Stations of the Cross is a spiritual practice that invites us to trace in prayer and contemplation fourteen moments of Christ's Passion, beginning with his condemnation to death and ending with his burial. These dramatic moments in Christ's Passion are captured in fourteen images that we find on the walls of most Catholic churches and in many places along outdoor pathways. The Stations are prayed either by a community or by individuals while standing before each station's image. At each station, a prayer is recited, usually a scripture passage is shared, and some brief meditation or reflection is read.

1. Jesus Is Condemned to Death

2. Jesus Takes Up His Cross

3. Jesus Falls the First Time

4. Jesus Meets His Mother

5. Simon Helps Jesus Carry the Cross

6. Veronica Wipes the Face of Jesus

7. Jesus Falls the Second Time

8. Jesus Meets the Women of Jerusalem

9.   Jesus Falls the Third Time

10. Jesus Is Stripped of His Garments

11. Jesus Is Nailed to the Cross

12. Jesus Dies on the Cross

13. Jesus Is Taken Down from the Cross

14. Jesus Is Laid in the Tomb

The Stations of the Cross for Married Couples

Begin by making the Sign of the Cross.
Lord Jesus Christ,
fill our hearts with the light of your Spirit,
so that by following you on your final journey
we may come to know the price of our redemption
and become worthy of a share
in the fruits of your Passion, Death, and
    Resurrection.
You who live and reign forever and ever.
Amen.

The First Station: Jesus Is Condemned to Death

Pray
We adore you, O Christ, and we bless you.

Genuflect
Because by your holy Cross
you have redeemed the world.

Rise

Read

"Once more Pilate went out and said to them, 'Look, I am bringing him out to you, so that you may know that I find no guilt in him.' . . . The Jews answered, 'We have a law, and according to that law he ought to die, because he made himself the Son of God'" (John 19:4, 7).

Reflect

Jesus was condemned even though he was innocent. In marriage we condemn our spouses whenever we judge or criticize them without seeking to understand what they do or say or when we ignore, dismiss, or downplay our spouses' point of view or how they feel. *Pause for reflection.*

Pray

Lord, help me be more respectful toward my spouse. Help me refrain from making judgmental assumptions about my spouse. Help me to listen so I can understand and, if I do not understand, ask for clarity, and only then respond.

Pray the Our Father together, and then pray:
Lord Jesus Christ,
Son of God,
have mercy on me, a sinner.

The Second Station: Jesus Takes Up His Cross

Pray
We adore you, O Christ, and we bless you.

Genuflect
Because by your holy Cross,
you have redeemed the world.

Rise

Read
"Then [Pilate] handed [Jesus] over to them to be crucified.
So they took Jesus, and carrying the cross himself he went out to what is called the Place of the Skull, in Hebrew, Golgotha" (John 19:16–17).

Reflect
Jesus carried his Cross to Golgotha, a painful and agonizing journey. Marriage brings many joys, but it has its crosses. We all have a cross to carry. Some of our crosses may come from our roles and responsibilities as husband, wife, father, mother, provider, protector, and teacher to children. As followers of Jesus, we need to be willing to recognize our crosses, embrace them, and carry them as he carried his. *Pause for reflection.*

Pray
Lord, give me the courage to carry my cross as you carried yours and to act responsibly and with

love toward my spouse and my children, especially when I don't feel like it.

Pray the Our Father together, and then pray:
Lord Jesus Christ,
Son of God,
have mercy on me, a sinner.

The Third Station: Jesus Falls for the First Time

Pray
We adore you, O Christ, and we bless you.

Genuflect
Because by your holy Cross,
you have redeemed the world.

Rise

Read
"We had all gone astray like sheep,
    all following our own way;
But the LORD laid upon him
    the guilt of us all" (Isaiah 53:6).

Reflect
Jesus falls under the weight of the Cross. In marriage we can easily fall under the weight of our
own unrealistic expectations—what we expect of
our spouses, of ourselves, and of our marriages.
Unrealistic expectations give us a false perception
of reality and set us up for unnecessary disap-
pointments. *Pause for reflection.*

Pray
Lord, help me be realistic in what I expect of my
spouse. Help me be honest with myself about
what marriage is. Help me accept that marriage
is a daily decision to dedicate myself to my spouse
out of self-giving love.

Pray the Our Father together, and then pray:
Lord Jesus Christ,
Son of God,
have mercy on me, a sinner.

The Fourth Station: Jesus Meets His Mother

Pray
We adore you, O Christ, and we bless you.

Genuflect
Because by your holy Cross,
you have redeemed the world.

Rise

Read
"Simeon blessed them and said to Mary his
mother, 'Behold, this child is destined for the fall
and rise of many in Israel, and to be a sign that
will be contradicted (and you yourself a sword
will pierce) so that the thoughts of many hearts
may be revealed'" (Luke 2:34–35).

Reflect

On the way to Calvary, Jesus sees his mother, Mary, and she sees her son in agony under the weight of the Cross. She must have suffered greatly. As husbands, wives, and parents we suffer when we see a spouse in pain, emotionally or physically, or when we see our children struggle with school or with friends. Like Mary, we can join our suffering with Jesus' saving suffering. *Pause for reflection.*

Pray

Lord, help me learn from Mary how to cope with suffering and sorrow and to understand the value of pain in life. Help me learn how to accept moments of discomfort as opportunities to join you in your suffering—as did Mary—for the redemption of humanity.

Pray the Our Father together, and then pray:
Lord Jesus Christ,
Son of God,
have mercy on me, a sinner.

The Fifth Station: Simon Helps Jesus Carry the Cross

Pray
We adore you, O Christ, and we bless you.

Genuflect
Because by your holy Cross,
you have redeemed the world.

Rise

Read
"They pressed into service a passer-by, Simon, a Cyrenian, who was coming in from the country, the father of Alexander and Rufus, to carry his cross" (Mark 15:21).

Reflect
At this fifth station, Simon is forced into helping Jesus carry the Cross. In marriage there are times when for the sake of our families we have to help carry one another's crosses. This is difficult, but the example of Simon invites us to carry our spouse's cross generously and gracefully. *Pause for reflection.*

Pray
Lord, give me the strength to carry my spouse's cross when it gets too heavy for them. Give me the courage to be generous and the strength to do so without complaining.

Pray the Our Father together, and then pray:
Lord Jesus Christ,
Son of God,
have mercy on me, a sinner.

The Sixth Station: Veronica Wipes the Face of Jesus

Pray
We adore you, O Christ, and we bless you.

Genuflect
Because by your holy Cross,
you have redeemed the world.

Rise

Read
"I gave my back to those who beat me,
    my cheeks to those who tore out my beard;
My face I did not hide
    from insults and spitting" (Isaiah 50:6).

Reflect
Jesus meets Veronica, who, in an act of compassion, steps out of the crowd to wipe Jesus' blood from his face. In marriage we are often called to be Veronica for our spouse. Life is difficult, and in the tough moments we must be willing to support, care for, and love our spouse with deep compassion. *Pause for reflection.*

Pray
Lord, help me be aware of and sensitive to the challenges my spouse is facing. Help me be ready and have the courage to set aside everything in order to wipe sweat and tears, to give comfort, and to stand by my spouse in moments of trial.

Pray the Our Father together, and then pray:
Lord Jesus Christ,
Son of God,
have mercy on me, a sinner.

The Seventh Station: Jesus Falls the Second Time

Pray
We adore you, O Christ, and we bless you.

Genuflect
Because by your holy Cross,
you have redeemed the world.

Rise

Read
"Though harshly treated, he submitted
        and did not open his mouth;
Like a lamb led to slaughter
        or a sheep silent before shearers,
        he did not open his mouth" (Isaiah 53:7).

Reflect
At this station we see Jesus fall again because of his exhaustion and the weight of the Cross. In marriage, when we fall, we may be tempted to make excuses for what we did or blame our spouse for our shortcomings. When Jesus fell, he did not blame us or complain that the Cross was too heavy. He accepted the suffering for us. *Pause for reflection.*

Pray
Lord, help me acknowledge my own mistakes and shortcomings without making excuses or blaming my spouse for the problems I create.

Help me recognize and accept my own failings
and brokenness and turn to you for healing.

Pray the Our Father together, and then pray:
Lord Jesus Christ,
Son of God,
have mercy on me, a sinner.

The Eight Station: Jesus Meets the Women of Jerusalem

Pray
We adore you, O Christ, and we bless you.

Genuflect
Because by your holy Cross,
you have redeemed the world.

Rise

Read
"A large crowd of people followed Jesus, including many women who mourned and lamented
him. Jesus turned to them and said, 'Daughters
of Jerusalem, do not weep for me; weep instead
for yourselves and for your children'" (Luke
23:27–28).

Reflect
On the way to Calvary, Jesus told a group of
women who were crying for him to cry instead
for themselves and for their children. In marriage
we can easily be distracted by the many activities

going on in our life. Jesus encourages us to keep our attention focused on what is most important: our marriage relationship. The Holy Spirit gives us strength, wisdom, and courage to overcome the challenges we face. *Pause for reflection.*

Pray
Lord, help me stay focused on what is most important in my life—my marriage. Help me make my spouse my daily priority in my life so that together we can face any challenge we may encounter.

Pray the Our Father together, and then pray:
Lord Jesus Christ,
Son of God,
have mercy on me, a sinner.

The Ninth Station: Jesus Falls the Third Time

Pray
We adore you, O Christ, and we bless you.

Genuflect
Because by your holy Cross,
you have redeemed the world.

Rise

Read
"Yet it was our pain that he bore,
    our sufferings he endured.
We thought of him as stricken,
    struck down by God and afflicted" (Isaiah 53:4).

Reflect

Jesus is exhausted and running out of energy.
The weight of the Cross is unbearable, and he
falls again. In marriage we fall each time that we
are unable to forgive and let our hurts pile up as
resentment grows. The weight of our anger weak-
ens our relationship and keeps us stuck, unable
to move forward. *Pause for reflection.*

Pray

Lord, give me the courage to tell my spouse that
I am sorry. Give my spouse the strength to let go
of the hurts caused by me. Help us both reach
an understanding about our differences and to
move forward without dwelling on each other's
past mistakes or bringing them up every time we
encounter a conflict.

Pray the Our Father together, and then pray:
Lord Jesus Christ,
Son of God,
have mercy on me, a sinner.

The Tenth Station: Jesus Is Stripped of His Garments

Pray
We adore you, O Christ, and we bless you.

Genuflect
Because by your holy Cross,
you have redeemed the world.

Rise

Read
"They took his clothes and divided them into four shares, a share for each soldier. They also took his tunic" (John 19:23).

Reflect
Jesus arrives at Calvary, and the soldiers strip him of his garments. In marriage we can unjustly strip our spouses of their dignity when we betray a confidence, when we criticize our spouse in front of our children, or when we speak unkindly about our spouses to our friends or coworkers. *Pause for reflection.*

Pray
Lord, help me control my mouth. At times it is very tempting to complain about my spouse in front of my children or our friends. I recognize that doing so damages our marriage. Give me the courage to tell my feelings to my spouse in private and to refrain from speaking ill of my spouse to others.

Pray the Our Father together, and then pray:
Lord Jesus Christ,
Son of God,
have mercy on me, a sinner.

The Eleventh Station: Jesus Is Nailed to the Cross

Pray
We adore you, O Christ, and we bless you.

Genuflect
Because by your holy Cross,
you have redeemed the world.

Rise

Read
"And when they came to a place called Golgotha (which means Place of the Skull), they gave Jesus wine to drink mixed with gall. But when he had tasted it, he refused to drink" (Matthew 27:33–34). "Then they crucified him and divided his garments by casting lots for them to see what each should take. It was nine o'clock in the morning when they crucified him" (Mark 15:24–25).

Reflect
At this station we recall Jesus being crucified with his mother watching. The soldiers pounded the nails in Jesus' hands and feet. In marriage there are times when we pound "death nails" into our relationship, often without realizing it. These nails are words said in anger, to get even, or out of jealousy. They are the choices we make out of selfishness. Each of these creates a barrier, puts distance between us, and does great damage to our marriage. *Pause for reflection.*

Pray

Lord, help me cherish my marriage, and help me
remember that my spouse is a gift given to me. Help
me remember this, especially when I am angry or
jealous or I am tempted to act selfishly. Help me,
Lord, build up my marriage with patience, generosity, kind words, and thoughtful actions.

Pray the Our Father together, and then pray:
Lord Jesus Christ,
Son of God,
have mercy on me, a sinner.

The Twelfth Station: Jesus Dies on the Cross

Pray
We adore you, O Christ, and we bless you.

Genuflect
Because by your holy Cross,
you have redeemed the world.

Rise

Read

"And at three o'clock Jesus cried out in a loud
voice, 'Eloi, Eloi, lema sabachthani?' which is
translated, 'My God, my God, why have you for-
saken me?' . . . Jesus gave a loud cry and breathed
his last." (Mark 15:34, 37)

Reflect
At this station we meditate on Jesus' death on the
Cross, his sacrifice for us. Jesus died for us so that

we may have life. Marriage demands sacrifices. For our marriages to grow, our egos must die a little. We must let go of some of our wants and preferences to make room for the needs and wants of our spouse. *Pause for reflection.*

Pray
Lord, help me to be more generous toward my spouse, to be flexible and adaptable. Give me the courage to make room for my spouse to grow and flourish as you so will. Help me make any needed sacrifices for us to be joyful together.

Pray the Our Father together, and then pray:
Lord Jesus Christ,
Son of God,
have mercy on me, a sinner.

The Thirteenth Station: Jesus Is Taken Down from the Cross

Pray
We adore you, O Christ, and we bless you.

Genuflect
Because by your holy Cross,
you have redeemed the world.

Rise

Read
"Now there was a virtuous and righteous man named Joseph who, though he was a member of the council, had not consented to their plan

of action. . . . He went to Pilate and asked for the body of Jesus. After he had taken the body down, he wrapped it in a linen cloth" (Luke 23:50, 52–53a).

Reflect

We are at a station filled with sorrow and loss. Mary and other disciples are present as Jesus is taken down from the Cross. In life every sacrifice brings sorrow and a sense of loss. A healthy marriage requires many sacrifices. Sometimes the pain of these losses may cause us to doubt. These are the times when we can turn to Mary who is a model of unwavering hope in the midst of immense sorrow and ask her for the grace of hope. *Pause for reflection.*

Pray

Lord, give me hope in the difficult moments of our marriage. Give me the strength to carry the weight of my spouse's humanity, and give my spouse the courage to carry mine. Give us the grace and the wisdom to see beyond our own imperfections.

Pray the Our Father together, and then pray:
Lord Jesus Christ,
Son of God,
have mercy on me, a sinner.

The Fourteenth Station: Jesus Is Laid in the Tomb

Pray

We adore you, O Christ, and we bless you.

Genuflect

Because by your holy Cross,
you have redeemed the world.

Rise

Read

"[He] laid him in a rock-hewn tomb in which no one had yet been buried. . . . The women who had come from Galilee with him followed behind, and when they had seen the tomb and the way in which his body was laid in it, they returned and prepared spices and perfumed oils" (Luke 23:53b, 55–56a).

Reflect

At this final station we meditate on Jesus' burial in the dark tomb. In every marriage there are days of darkness, like in a tomb. These are times when we do not know where we are going; we feel numb, sad, confused, and discouraged. Those may have been the feelings of Mary and the disciples as they laid Jesus in the tomb. But when dawn came on the third day, they found new life in the Risen Christ. *Pause for reflection.*

Pray

Lord, during our days of darkness, be our light.
Help us remember that you rose from the tomb,

and because of it, with your grace you bring light to our marriage. Guide us with your Spirit. Then a new day will dawn and joy will return to our home.

Pray the Our Father together, and then pray:
Lord Jesus Christ,
Son of God,
have mercy on me, a sinner.

The Angelus

This devotional prayer has been prayed for centuries in churches, convents, and monasteries three times a day: at sunrise, at noon, and at sunset. It is often accompanied by the ringing of church bells as a call to prayer for the whole community. Some Catholic parishes still practice this devotion, and families pray it at home. The Angelus is generally prayed while standing.

I (John) remember that when I was growing up in Italy, I would be able to tell the time by the ringing of the morning, noon, and evening Angelus bells. My brother and I often fought for the privilege of going to the parish to help the sacristan ring the bells. Years later, the ringing of the bells became automated, but the prayer practice continues to this day in my hometown.

The beginning of this prayer has its origin in the monasteries of Italy in the eleventh and twelfth centuries. In 1956, Pope Pius XII asked the faithful throughout the world to pray the Angelus for the persecuted Christians in the East.

In Rome there is a tradition of reciting the Angelus with the pope. Each Sunday at noon, the pope goes to the window of his apartment in the Vatican overlooking St. Peter's Square and recites the Angelus with the pilgrims who are present. During the Easter season, the Church prays a similar prayer, the Regina Coeli (see page 59), instead of the Angelus.

V. The angel of the Lord declared unto Mary.
R. And she conceived of the Holy Spirit.

Recite one Hail Mary.
V. Behold the handmaid of the Lord.
R. Be it done unto me according to thy word.

Recite one Hail Mary.
V. And the Word was made flesh.
R. And dwelt among us.

Recite one Hail Mary.
V. Pray for us, O holy Mother of God.
R. That we may be made worthy of the promises
  of Christ.

Let us pray:
Pour forth, we beseech thee, O Lord, thy grace
  into our hearts,
that we, to whom the Incarnation of Christ, thy Son,
was made known by the message of an angel,
may, by his Passion and Cross,
be brought to the glory of his Resurrection.
Through the same Christ, our Lord.
Amen.

This prayer is composed of three biblically inspired verses narrating how the Incarnation came about. It is often recited with one person saying one line and everyone else present responding with the second line.

The Advent Wreath

Beginning four Sundays before Christmas, Catholics observe the season of Advent, which is a time of waiting for the coming of Christ. The First Sunday of Advent marks the beginning of a new liturgical year. A traditional way of celebrating this season is to pray with the Advent wreath, a circle of greenery with four candles. Three of the candles are purple (violet) to remind us of our call to return to God during the season, and one is pink (rose) to remind us of the intense joy we as Christians know. Each week, beginning on Sunday, an additional candle is lit while a prayer is said. The first week, we light a purple candle, the second week we light two purple candles, the third week we light two purple candles and the pink candle, and the fourth week we light all four candles. The candles are lit every day, usually in the evening or anytime prayers are said.

The Advent wreath has been a tradition for John and me from the beginning of our marriage. We married in November, and among the wedding gifts we received was an Advent wreath. A thoughtful couple who felt strongly about the importance of praying as a family on various occasions gave us the gift. We have used it every Advent since. During Advent the wreath sits in the center of our kitchen table, and we light it each evening before dinner. The most memorable times of praying as a family with the Advent wreath were the years when our daughters were young. This ritual involved lively discussions about whose turn it was to light and blow out the candles.

Advent Wreath Prayer

O Lord, our God,
at this time of the year when daylight is short
we prepare to celebrate Jesus, the true light,
coming into the world.

Each week as we light another candle
and our wreath becomes brighter,
fill our home with the light of Christ.
Light the candle(s).

Lord,
bless our Advent wreath,
and as we light the candle(s),
we ask that you shine your light on our families
     and friends,
and everyone else, especially those in most need
     of your help.
We also pray for . . . [those present mention the
needs or the people for whom they want to pray].

Lord, help us to be the light of Christ for those we
     meet each day in all we do and say.

With grateful hearts we pray:
Glory be to the Father, and to the Son, and to the
     Holy Spirit,
as it was in the beginning, is now, and ever shall be,
world without end.
Amen.

O Antiphons of Advent

When I (John) was a young child, I loved Christmas, as most children do. In Italy, we did not have Santa Claus, but instead during Advent we waited for Baby Jesus to make our Christmas wishes come true. That seems to be a different world from ours today. The commercialization of the holidays distracts us from the true meaning of Christmas.

I remember fondly the last days before Christmas when I was growing up. In the early evenings I would walk with my family to the nearby church for Vespers (Evening Prayer). I remember walking at times in the snow, at times in the chilly air of clear December nights, looking at the store windows and dreaming about the gifts I wanted. I also remember the mood in the church. It was joyful—full of light and resounding with beautiful music.

As I grew up, I learned that Advent was a time of waiting for the coming of Jesus, and we would express our hope for his coming through the singing of special antiphons during Vespers. Antiphons are verses that are recited or sung before and after a psalm or a canticle. The antiphons for this time of waiting are called O Antiphons because they all begin with the invocation "O." The verses are beautiful poetry that use imagery from the Old Testament to remind us that Jesus is the fulfillment of God's promises. He is the gift we are waiting for. These prayers begin on December 17 and end on December 23.

December 17

O Wisdom of our God Most High,
guiding creation with power and love:
come to teach us the path of knowledge!

December 18

O Leader of the House of Israel,
Giver of the Law to Moses on Sinai:
come to rescue us with your mighty power!

December 19

O Root of Jesse's stem,
sign of God's love for all his people:
come to save us without delay!

December 20

O Key of David,
opening the gates of God's eternal kingdom:
come and free the prisoners of darkness!

December 21

O Radiant Dawn,
splendor of eternal light, sun of justice:
come and shine on those who dwell in darkness
and in the shadow of death.

December 22

O King of all nations and keystone of the Church:
come and save man, whom you formed from the
dust!

December 23

O Emmanuel, our King and Giver of Law:
come to save us, Lord our God!

Even if you are not praying the Liturgy of the Hours, you can still make the praying of these antiphons a part of your Advent traditions. You can read each one of these antiphons on the assigned date when you light the candles of your Advent wreath (see page 119), or you can pray them in front of the Christmas tree or your nativity scene before going to bed.

Eucharistic Adoration

Eucharistic adoration is a devotion that was part of both our childhoods, and it is something in which we now regularly participate as a couple at our parish. Eucharistic adoration is the practice of praying in front of the exposed Blessed Sacrament at a time other than during Mass. The Church encourages this devotion because the Eucharist is central in the life of a Christian.

If you have never participated in eucharistic adoration, here is what you can expect to see and experience when you go: The priest or deacon processes into the church and takes a large consecrated host from the tabernacle and places it in a special vessel, a monstrance, that allows for everyone to easily see the Blessed Sacrament. The ritual of exposing the Blessed Sacrament includes prayers, singing, and the use of incense. Incense symbolizes our prayers rising up to heaven. Then the priest or deacon may read a passage from scripture and offer words of reflection that invite those attending to recognize Christ's presence in their lives and to grow in appreciation of the eucharistic mystery. This is followed by a time of adoration spent in silent reflection and prayer.

One of the common prayers read by the celebrant at the end of eucharistic adoration helps us remember the purpose of this devotion:

Lord Jesus Christ,
you gave us the Eucharist

as the memorial of your suffering and death.
May our worship of this sacrament of your Body
    and Blood
help us to experience the salvation you won for us
and the peace of the kingdom
where you live with the Father
and the Holy Spirit,
one God, forever and ever. Amen.

The period of adoration concludes with the priest or deacon blessing those assembled with the Blessed Sacrament, by holding up the monstrance and making the Sign of the Cross with it, and then returning the host to the tabernacle. The hour concludes with a prayer of praise and a song.

Different parishes have different customs around this devotion. For example, in our parish we have a monthly holy hour, which is one hour of eucharistic adoration. During Advent and Lent, we celebrate the Forty Hours' Devotion. This is eucharistic adoration that lasts for forty consecutive hours, and parishioners sign up to be present at different intervals. Someone is always present, day and night. The forty hours represent the time during which Christ's body remained in the tomb. The practice of the Forty Hours' Devotion is only several centuries old, but the Church has had a long tradition of praying in front of the exposed consecrated host, dating back to the early centuries. There are also parishes that in recent years have received permission to have the Blessed Sacrament exposed for twenty-four hours continuously, day after day. This practice is called perpetual adoration.

Parishioners take turns spending time with Christ in the Eucharist to pray for the Church and their needs and to grow in their relationship with him.

John and I participate in both the monthly holy hour and the biannual Forty Hours' Devotion offered by our parish. These are moments when we can go to church and spend time with Christ in the Blessed Sacrament. We sit and kneel together quietly in prayer, and our worries and busy lives are intentionally suspended.

Visits to the Blessed Sacrament are another common Catholic practice that is an extension of eucharistic adoration. This is a simpler devotional practice, and it is often done by oneself. To make such a visit requires only quiet, private prayer in front of the tabernacle in a church. There are no formal prayers, hymns, or gestures involved, simply one's attention, time, and humble prayer before Christ present in the reserved sacrament.

Chaplet of Divine Mercy

The Chaplet of Divine Mercy is a Catholic devotion based on the apparitions of Jesus to St. Faustina Kowalska in the 1930s. St. Faustina was a Polish religious sister who was declared a saint in 2000. St. Faustina reported having received this prayer, the Chaplet of Divine Mercy, through visions and conversations with Jesus. It is prayed following the style of the Rosary, using the same beads.

In her diary, Faustina wrote that Jesus asked her to pray the Chaplet and to encourage others to do so. The Chaplet has a threefold purpose: to obtain mercy, to express trust in Christ's mercy, and to show mercy to others. It can be said at any time, but it is particularly appropriate on Divine Mercy Sunday, which is celebrated on the Second Sunday of Easter. The Chaplet is also commonly prayed on Fridays at 3:00 p.m., the hour in which Jesus died on the Cross.

How to Pray the Chaplet of Divine Mercy Using the Rosary Beads

1. Using the crucifix of the rosary, make the Sign of the Cross.

2. On the first bead after the crucifix, pray: "You expired, Jesus, but the source of life gushed forth for souls, and the ocean of mercy opened up for the whole world. O Fount of Life, unfathomable

Divine Mercy, envelop the whole world and empty Yourself out upon us."

3.   Then repeat three times the following prayer: "O Blood and Water, which gushed forth from the Heart of Jesus as a fountain of mercy for us, I trust in You!"

4.   On the next bead, pray the Our Father (see page 34).

5.   On the next bead, pray the Hail Mary (see page 35).

6.   On the next bead, pray the Apostles' Creed (see pages 36–37).

7.   On the large bead of each decade, pray: "Eternal Father, I offer you the Body and Blood, Soul and Divinity, of your Dearly Beloved Son, Our Lord, Jesus Christ, in atonement for our sins and those of the whole world."

8.   On each of the ten small beads, pray: "For the sake of his sorrowful Passion, have mercy on us and on the whole world."

9.   After praying five decades, pray the following prayer three times: "Holy God, Holy Mighty One, Holy Immortal One, have mercy on us and on the whole world."

10. Then pray this closing prayer: "Eternal God, in whom mercy is endless and the treasury of compassion inexhaustible, look kindly upon us and

increase your mercy in us, that in difficult moments we might not despair nor become despondent, but with great confidence submit ourselves to your holy will, which is Love and Mercy itself. Amen."

Novenas

Novenas are an ancient form of prayer that consist of praying for nine consecutive days, weeks, months, or other units of time in preparation for a particular event or for a specific need or intention. According to Church tradition, the first novena was the novena to the Holy Spirit. It was prayed by the Blessed Mother and the apostles after the Ascension of Jesus. They returned to Jerusalem and waited in prayer in the upper room for the coming of the Holy Spirit on Pentecost. Today, the Church still commemorates that event with a Novena to the Holy Spirit, which is prayed between the Feasts of the Ascension and Pentecost.

The devotion of praying novenas is deeply rooted in my (Teri's) family. When I was growing up, a favorite novena in my family was to Blessed Martin de Porres, who at the time was not yet a saint. Martin de Porres was a Dominican brother who lived in Lima, Peru, in the seventeenth century; he was canonized in 1962.

Novenas are not magic incantations to help us obtain anything we want. Catholics pray to Mary and to the saints for their intercession with the understanding that through their prayers on our behalf, God will give us what is truly good for us, not just what we want because we want it or think we need it.

You can find many novenas to Mary and the saints online or at your Catholic bookstore. However, we are not suggesting that you just pick any novena to pray.

Novenas should flow from a personal relationship we develop with Mary or a particular saint. In the Catholic Church we are blessed with a very diverse and rich family of saints who stand by us ready to help us, like older brothers and sisters. Learn about them, and invite them into your life and your family. Then, in the context of those spiritual relationships, praying to the saints makes sense. It is a way to live and celebrate what we believe and call the Communion of Saints.

Among the novenas used by our family, one that we have used often during our relocations has been the Novena to St. Joseph. There are several prayers that can be used as novenas to St. Joseph. The one below is the simplest and dates back to the sixteenth century. Recite it for nine days.

Novena to St. Joseph

O St. Joseph, whose protection is so great,
so strong, so prompt before the throne of God,
I place in you all my interests and desires.
O St. Joseph, do assist me
by your powerful intercession
and obtain for me from your Divine Son
all spiritual blessings through Jesus Christ,
Our Lord;
so that having engaged here below
your heavenly power,
I may offer my thanksgiving and homage
to the most loving of fathers.

O St. Joseph, I never weary contemplating you
with Jesus asleep in your arms;
I dare not approach
while he reposes near your heart.
Press him in my name
and kiss his fine head for me,
and ask him to return the kiss
when I draw my dying breath.

St. Joseph, pray for us.
[Mention aloud your personal intentions.]

Amen.

Acknowledgments

The publisher gratefully acknowledges the following sources from which portions of this book were compiled. Every effort has been made to give proper acknowledgment to authors and copyright holders of the texts herein. If any omissions or errors have been made, please notify the publisher who will correct it in future editions.

Edizioni San Paolo s.r.l. "Prayer of Cardinal Bergoglio," A prayer to Mary the untier of knots, distributed with the imprimatur of the Archbishop of Buenos Aires, Monsignor Bergoglio, *Our Lady Untier of Knots: Story of a Marian Devotion* by Miguel Cuartero Samperi © 2014.

Preghiera a Maria che scioglie i nodi diffusa con l'imprimatur dell'allora arcivescovo di Buenos Aires monsignor Bergoglio, in Miguel Cuartero Samperi, *Nostra Signora che scioglie i nodi. Storia di una devozione mariana*, © 2014.

Edizioni San Paolo s.r.l.

Piazza Soncino 5 – 20092 Cinisello Balsamo (Milano) Italia

Additional Prayer Resources

We hope that this simple prayer book is helpful to you and that here is the place you go to when you want to find prayers to teach to your little ones one day should you be blessed with children. As you grow in your marriage and you mature spiritually you may desire other prayer resources to fill your spiritual needs. The following books may be helpful to you.

Amazing Grace: The Blessings of Sacramentals by Julie Dortch Cragon

Bless My Child: A Catholic Mother's Prayer Book by Julie Cragon

Catholic Household Blessings and Prayers by Bishops' Committee on the Liturgy, United States Conference of Catholic Bishops

The Catholic Mom's Prayer Companion: A Book of Daily Reflections by Lisa M. Hendey and Sarah A. Reinhard

Feeding Your Family's Soul: Dinner Table Spirituality by Donna-Marie Cooper O'Boyle

Paths to Prayer: A Field Guide to Ten Catholic Traditions by Pat Fosarelli

Pray with Me: Seven Simple Ways to Pray With Your Children by Grace Mazza Urbanski

Prayers for the Domestic Church: A Handbook for Worship in the Home by Edward M. Hays

A Psalter for Couples by Pierre-Marie Dumont

Talking to God: Prayers for Catholic Women by Julie Dortch Cragon

We Celebrate Our Marriage: Heartfelt Prayers of Love by John Van Bemmel and Lauri Van Bemmel

John and Teri Bosio are active in parish and family ministry, serving parishes and dioceses around the country. The Bosios lead couples' retreats and workshops on family ministry for deacons and priests. They wrote *Joined By Grace*, a marriage preparation program from Ave Maria Press, and produced two parish-based marriage enrichment programs: *Six Dates for Catholic Couples* and *The Beatitudes: A Couple's Path to Greater Joy*. They are the authors of several books, including *Happy Together* and *Blessed Is Marriage*.

AVE MARIA PRESS

Founded in 1865, Ave Maria Press,
a ministry of the Congregation of
Holy Cross, is a Catholic publishing
company that serves the spiritual and
formative needs of the Church and its
schools, institutions, and ministers;
Christian individuals and families; and
others seeking spiritual nourishment.

For a complete listing of titles from

Ave Maria Press

Sorin Books

Forest of Peace

Christian Classics

visit www.avemariapress.com

AVE MARIA PRESS
Notre Dame, IN
A Ministry of the United States Province of Holy Cross